KU-163-568

Contents

Introduction

In the colloquium series of the Center for European Studies, the fiftieth anniversary of the Nazi seizure of power had certainly to be a compelling subject. Between January 30, 1933, when Hitler was named Chancellor of the Reich and March 23, when the Reichstag voted him almost complete power, the National Socialists grasped at dictatorial control with amazing rapidity. Within a year the dissolution of political parties and free trade unions, the remoulding of German federalism, the initial purges of Jews and arrests of political opponents quickly transformed Germany into an ideologically regimented, authoritarian state. How did this process develop? Who pushed it forward, who acquiesced, who resisted? What was the nature of the system that entrenched itself? How did inherited structures, whether those of state and bureaucracy, or those of family and civil society, adjust? Despite a massive literature, questions such as these still search for answers.

Earlier Center colloquia have exploited historical anniversaries to reconsider key events in recent European history. Students of France reviewed the role of Charles de Gaulle in 1979 on the occasion of the tenth anniversary of his death. A Center conference in 1980 considered recent findings and interpretations of the Fall of France, and in the spring of 1982 a gathering of participants and scholars met to discuss the Marshall Plan on the thirty-fifth anniversary of Marshall's famous address in June 1947. That colloquium has now appeared as The Marshall Plan: A Retrospective, the first volume in a series published by Westview Press. The proceedings published here form the second volume in the series. We are hopeful that some of the other colloquia held since "The Nazi Rise to Power"--including symposia on the emigration of German social science to America in the 1930's and on the First World War--will also be published in this format.

The Center's colloquia have all been organized to permit a maximum of informed discussion. Each session begins with a summary of the ideas and themes of papers written for the colloquium. These form the bases of the essays published here. They are designed not as substantive reports, but as outlines of historical controversy or recent advances in scholarship. Most of the colloquium time is devoted to open discussion among the fifty or so participants. The discussions are summarized with occasional quotation in the volumes. Participants include expert scholars along with interested non-specialists. The mix has ensured that the colloquia have served both to debate the most recent historical arguments and to take stock of accumulated interpretations. The present volume, we believe, certainly carries out both these tasks and should interest specialists and the "lay reader" alike.

The organizers of the colloquium decided at the outset that to survey the entire Nazi experience was impossible within the format of a weekend conference. Instead it was decided to focus on problems relating to the Nazi rise to power and the nature of the regime that they imposed. Since time was brief, and the colloquium assembled many of the scholars who have contributed some of the leading studies, the organizers tried to move discussion quickly into the questions that still seemed unresolved. This introduction will seek to identify the historiographical issues that were set to participants.

The first session dealt with the collapse of Weimar. Recent work has focused on different aspects of this complex process. On the one hand, scholars have tried to explore the failure of the Republic as a breakdown of consensus among representatives of Germany's powerful interest groups or other elites. As a democracy Weimar was distinguished from the Third French Republic, the United States congressional system, and British cabinet government by a combination of elements. Religious cleavages persisted alongside social-class divisions. Even within the Protestant middle classes, even before the advent of Nazism, at least three ideological families found their preferences hard to reconcile. Proportional representation made political parties the fundamental units of governance, endowed party leaders with the important capacity to allocate safe seats and thus strengthen discipline within, but likewise compelled them to participate in exhausting coalition negotiations. The party system further tended toward a symbiotic relationship with organized interest groups--preeminently labor unions, the trade associations of heavy industry, East Elbian landlords, but also smaller farmers and wine growers of the South and West, veterans, bureaucrats, associations of mortgage holders, etc.--who to varying degrees could exert strong political leverage. Finally, the independently elected Reich President had the power to shape or even to bypass parliamentary majorities, but his office was itself subject to the competing claims of traditionally influential groups, such as the military or bureaucratic leadership. If these elites remained stalemated, then their deadlock helped to paralyze public decision-making in general.

Two of the participants in the first panel had explored these relationships among organized interests. Henry Turner's recent book focuses on the patterns of heavy-industry's financing of political parties, among them the Nazis.[1] Turner has sought to modify earlier notions of occult financial support for Hitler's party. He has stressed instead the hesitations on the part of businessmen, their subventions to diverse political groupings, and the effort to keep a Nazi government at bay. In contrast, David Abraham has argued in his work that because the economic elites of Weimar could not agree on a common program that would allow stable conservative parliamentary rule, some of their members clearly sought authoritarian solutions, even if by 1932 these had to give a large voice to Hitler's party.[2]

To focus on the paralysis of the Weimar "system" provides only one analytical approach to the collapse of the Republic. The other major one involves investigating the mass movement that would replace the Republic. Twenty years ago William Sheridan Allen broke new ground by examining the National Socialist conquest at the local level.[3] For his colloquium contribution Allen was asked to reflect on his findings and summarize the process of National Socialist victory. What he has chosen to emphasize is how remarkable it would have been had the Weimar Republic not collapsed. His essay usefully summarizes the almost overwhelming sources of vulnerability. On the other hand, it is worth recalling that as of 1929 many qualified observers believed the Republic was well established. Despite the deep divisions revealed by the laborious coalition negotiations of 1928 and a bitter conflict in the Ruhr iron and steel industry, the regime did not seem in danger. Only the radicalization of the electorate during the Depression allowed a plausible alternative to emerge. To understand this phenomenon, the colloquium organizers asked Richard Hamilton to discuss the findings and methods of his recent study of Nazi voters.

Hitler's appointment as Chancellor may have finally been arranged by the bureaucratic entourage of President Hindenburg; nonetheless, despite a decline in votes in late 1932, his party possessed a clear Reichstag plurality (196 out of 584 delegates). Analyzing the sources of the electoral groundswell from 1930 to 1932, Hamilton has contested the older view, rooted in prewar Marxian analysis, but popularized later by

→ Seymour Martin Lipset and others, that Nazi support was
predominantly "petty-bourgeois." He has stressed
instead, first, variables that were already known--the
Protestant and rural mass support for the movement--and,
second, the electoral appeal to the upper-class. In
light of Hamilton's findings as well as those of other
researchers, including the work of Thomas Childers, who
also participated in the colloquium discussion, Nazism
appears as far less class-specific than it may have
earlier and far broader a protest.[4] Only reservoirs
of committed "confessional" voters, with entrenched
Roman Catholic or Marxist loyalties, remained immune as
groups.[5] Still, evaluation of the new findings is
subject to lively controversies concerning statistical
methods. Moreover, the construction of a historical
synthesis that takes account of a stalemate among
elites, on one level, and the electoral groundswell for
the Nazis on another, persists as a difficult problem.
The first panel was constructed to get at these open
issues. Of the opening statements, we include here
those of David Abraham and William Sheridan Allen. We
regret that Henry Turner and Richard Hamilton declined
to have their initial comments published in this
collection.

The second session sought to get at the difficult
issue of what typologies might be applied to the new
Nazi elite, their beliefs and their system of rule. The
issue of totalitarianism came up again in the following
discussion, but Saul Friedländer broached it here as
well when he emphasized the centrality of anti-Semitism.
For Friedländer anti-Semitism remains an irreducible
priority of Nazi ideology. It represented an end in
itself, not just a form of anti-Bolshevism, and not a
property of fascism in general. For Friedländer this
basic irreducibility means that no general typology such
as "fascism" or "totalitarianism" adequately accounts
for Nazism. While Friedländer insists on the historical
uniqueness of National Socialism, Jeffrey Herf tries to
depict this uniqueness more revealingly than conventional formulations often allowed. To be sure, Herf
suggests, ideology was central and not to be minimized
in importance. But, despite many analyses, the ideology
was not simply a rejection of modernity. Rather it
fused a supposely pre-modern yearning for "wholeness"
with a highly modern fascination with technology.

Michael Kater's contribution shifts ground.
Drawing upon his longer work on the social composition
and attitudes of the Nazi Party,[6] Kater presents a
portrait of a leadership of ambitious, successful
careerists--not at all marginals or misfits--which he
contrasted with the more brawling "lower middle-class"
mentality of the pre-1933 "old fighters." For Kater,
the result was a fusion of rational, bureaucratic styles
with the earlier militant commitments to leadership,

loyalty, and ideological fervor. Whether these "pure" Nazi values could appropriately be labelled petty bourgeois was contested in discussion.

Taking together the contributions of Allen, Herf, Kater, and Friedländer, as well as comments from the floor, the reader can discern the outline of a new picture of the Nazi movement and regime. Scholars have modified older categories imposed in larger part by the generation that had to grope for understanding as it was dispersed by Nazi brutality. The continuities between National Socialism and the political Right as conventionally understood, the temptation to compartmentalize Nazi values as "lower middle-class," or to fall back on a general model of fascism, these contributions suggest, must be significantly overhauled. Recent work indicates instead that Nazism appealed to broad and diverse strata of the German electorate; it was implanted by hard organizational work; it could incorporate the technological enthusiasm of the engineers even as its spokesmen seemed to hanker after old Gemeinschaften. Taken as a group the contributions here epitomize a stage of revision, when it is clear that old paradigms must crumble before new syntheses can be attempted.

Jane Caplan's and Michael Geyer's contributions take us to the center of the two major debates concerning the nature of National Socialist rule. This controversy opposes those who have been characterized by the opposing participants as "functionalist" and "intentionalist."[7] The functionalist position implies that Nazi policies represented the cumulative result of bureaucratic in-fighting and were not fully conceived in advance. The dynamic of administrative rivalries and flux served often to radicalize policies, and allowed Hitler to exploit his talents for brilliant opportunism and improvisation, even as he often sought to evade harsh decisions. The intentionalists believe this position is inadequate to explain, above all, foreign policy and genocide. They ascribe policy outcomes to the clear impetus of Hitler (or perhaps the narrow policy circle around him), motivated above all by ideological conviction. For many interpreters, including Friedländer, the idea of functionalism necessarily trivializes the Nazi commitment to anti-Semitic terror and to the project of exterminating the Jews. Defenders of functionalism argue that the horror of the Holocaust is not diminished by envisaging the "final solution" as the upshot of incremental decisions or bureaucratic ambition as well as an underlying anti-Semitism. (This debate is not the same as the argument whether it was Hitler or Himmler or other close advisers who were primarily resolved to murder the Jews. The question is whether the murder of the Jews was a policy goal from the outset of power or whether the full project emerged only as other half-way "solutions" were ruled out.)[8]

The argument between functionalists and intentionalists encompasses the specific debate concerning "polycracy" and the nature of Nazi totalitarianism. The
issue of polycracy focuses above all on the structure of
the regime and how it generated policies. Did the Nazi
regime consist of quasi-baronial fiefs, whose leaders
were determined to maximize their independence and
contributed to a regime that despite the appearances of
absolute control by the Führer had little central
coherence? The opponents of a polycratic view often
insist on the usefulness of the older idea of "totalitarianism" with its notion that power was clearly
monopolized at the center.[9]

These overlapping debates have helped to generate
research on the Nazi state and its agencies; however,
the terms proposed seem unnecessarily polarized.
Defenders of the concept of totalitarianism argued in
discussion that to demonstrate that infighting was rife
among the Nazi leadership does not mean that the regime
lacked the desire to impose total control. Totalitarianism need not imply monolithic coherence, but the
determination to monopolize the resources of power and
culture and prevent alternative leaders or political
ideas from having any influence. In this sense the
regime was totalitarian even while its leaders were
often locked in conflict. In the edited version of her
paper, Jane Caplan proposes that "structuralism" might
best express the fragmented nature of the regime without
suggesting that it was impossible to muster decisive
power at the center. Geyer suggests that control of
political power was crucial, but itself had to be fought
over.

If totalitarianism must be measured, however, by
how much control was actually achieved, then the
question of how totalitarian the regime was still
remains, not because the bureaucratic infighting was
endemic, but because interstices of power persisted.
The issue of how total control could be and the degree
to which it might be evaded underlies the next set of
papers. They focus, however, not on the power of the
regime per se, but on the degrees of enthusiasm,
acquiescence, resistance on the part of those governed.
Many historians have become clearly more comfortable
with the notion that an intermediate form of unwilling
acceptance lay between enthusiasm or even acquiescence,
and clandestine opposition work. For a long time after
the war, the term "internal emigration" was applied to
those who sought refuge in private life, harboring their
thoughts and unhappiness. But even as Klaus Tenfelde's
paper explains how mining communities could hold out
against giving wholesale assent to the new rulers and
seek to preserve the fabric of allegiance they had
before 1933, he cautions against broadening the notion
of resistance too far.

Almost every visitor who has talked with Germans of the period has met those whose families courted the displeasure of local Gauleiters or petty enthusiasts by refusing to give the Hitler salute or to participate in rallies, or by starting conspicuous church attendance, or even flouting the new social rituals such as the weekly lentil stew (Eintopf). It is certainly important to understand these withdrawals from Nazism's civic culture. But Tenfelde valuably cautions against broadening all such retreats into a concept of Resistance, which he wishes to reserve for politically motivated defiance at the cost of real personal risk.

The essays by Anson Rabinbach and Claudia Koonz explore this twilight domain of withdrawal, whether the thirst for reading or just plain privacy among the women whose survey data Rabinbach has unearthed or the disillusionment felt by Catholic and Protestant women, who, according to Koonz, originally hoped they might find more scope for female autonomy and organization under the National Socialist regime. (Focusing conversely on the lack of militant resistance among the working class, Mary Nolan's contribution points to earlier disorganization and disillusionment brought about by the rationalization of factory work.)

The colloquium passed from discussions of culture and society to those of foreign relations. Here the focus shifted to the responses to National Socialism abroad. Edward Bennett suggests how difficult it was for foreign statesmen and observers to understand the Nazi objectives, while Joseph Rovan's paper illustrates the early barriers to an effective anti-Nazi strategy on the part of the French Socialists committed as they were to ideals of disarmament. The discussion of foreign policy turned primarily, however, on the oral presentation of Stephen Schuker's exposition of Chamberlin's thinking, and the rationality of appeasement.

The essays in this volume demonstrate how in the course of half a century of anguished historical debate the issues have evolved, but yet how many problems persist. At least three orders of questions remain important. The first order concerns what happened or who believed what or supported which policies. While new research or documentation helps answer these questions, it can never exhaustively resolve them. For the second order of questions concerns "significance." What did it mean to hold a certain belief: from what point did obsessive anti-Semitism mean one sought to kill as many Jews as possible? Did women's thirst for privacy imply a latent resistance stance or not? Was it dangerous for the aspirations of the regime, or might it have served as a safety valve? A third order of questions involves the adequacy of terminology. Was the regime "totalitarian?" What does it mean to say it was

"polycratic?" Debates about terminology can be
frustrating in that they lead away from history into a
realm of formalism. On the other hand, they can
encourage a search for relevant evidence that expands
historical consciousness. The challenge is to exploit
the controversies for substantive research and
reflection and then know when to move on. But the
difficulty remains that almost every interesting
historical issue raises all three orders of questions
at once, hence the fascination and challenge.

There is a further challenge that this historical
colloquium exemplifies. That is the challenge of
causality. The question, for example, of why the Weimar
Republic collapsed has been "unpacked" to reveal
interlocking questions over the nature of the German
elites, many of whom wanted it to collapse, and the
sources of grass-roots rejection. The way most
historians have traditionally handled such disputes is
to insist on multicausality and the complexity of
factors behind all historical developments. Certain
works of synthesis, preeminently Karl Bracher's German
Dictatorship, represent splendid applications of this
multicausal approach. But an explanatory model based
upon aggregation may not suffice. This does not mean
that the alternative must be to insist on one sort of
causality, say class or interest group conflict, or
popular impatience with career politicians. Rather, a
survey of the contributions included here suggests that
our model of historical causality itself remains
problematic.

The model of causality is problematic at several
levels. It is problematic because, on the one hand, the
causes of great events never seem determinative enough.
On the psychological or moral level, events seem to
outrun causes reciting all the handicaps of German
politics and society still does not adequately account
for Auschwitz. Causality is problematic, on the other
hand, because it is over-determinative (not in the
Althusserian sense, but in the mathematical sense). The
historian can provide several causal matrices, each of
which can "explain" an outcome. When historians notice
this, the usual result is a fruitless argument over
whether, for instance ideological causes are more
important than political or economic, etc. The third
difficulty is that the role of generalization in history
still remains and must remain contested.

This colloquium, for example, brought together, on
one side, historians and social scientists who seek a
general typology for even what must forever count as one
of the most appalling of human experiences. The
typologies proposed are sometimes those of social
cleavages and their effect on politics, sometimes
psychological and moral categories of obedience,
acquiescence, enthusiasm or rejection. On the other

side the colloquium also included those who essentially
claim that the typologies are inadequate. Some of these
participants quarreled more with particular typologies,
such as Hamilton's critique of the lower middle-class
model of Nazi support, more than with the general effort
to derive such models. But others contested the very
effort to resort to any typology, as did Friedländer,
who argues that none is adequate to capture what Nazism
was about. Debates such as these are not easily
resolved. Max Weber designed ideal types, after all, to
provide a means for generalizing or placing within a
wider interpretative context, events that were
historically unique. But as the discussion at this
colloquim suggested, for some historians the searing
uniqueness of National Socialism precludes the
application of any ideal types. For others, no event
can be comprehended without the at least implicit
comparison that an ideal type provides.

These different approaches to historical phenomena
form as fundamental a division as political and
ideological preferences. Sometimes indeed they often
represent another facet of ideological differences. But
they also testify to different attitudes: perhaps a fear
of trivializing terrible history on the part of those
who distrust generalization, perhaps the fear of not
really assimilating its lessons on the part of those who
search for ideal types. In any case the two approaches
cannot simply be bridged or even "transcended." They
will remain as alternative modes of coming to terms with
the historical past. That is one reason why the papers
here can summarize debates and signal new departures,
but cannot close the issues.

**

The Center for European Studies is happy to
acknowledge grants from the French government and the
Federal Republic of Germany that enabled us to bring
participants from Europe. The editors of this volume
and planners of the colloquium are deeply indebted once
again to Abby Collins and the staff of the Center, who
bore the considerable organizational burden for the
colloquium with extraordinary (though customary)
competence and enthusiasm. Stephen Hubbell, who saw the
book through its final editorial stages also deserves
acknowledgment and thanks.

Charles S. Maier

Notes

1. Henry Ashby Turner, Jr., German Big Business and the Rise of Hitler (New York: Oxford University Press, 1985).

2. David Abraham, The Collapse of the Weimar Republic: Political Economy and Crisis (Princeton: Princeton University Press, 1981).

3. William Sheridan Allen, The Nazi Seizure of Power: The Experience of a Single German Town 1922-1945, revised edition (New York: Franklin Watts, 1984).

4. Richard F. Hamilton, Who Voted for Hitler? (Princeton: Princeton University Press, 1982); Thomas Childers, The Nazi Voter: The Social Foundations of Fascism in Germany, 1919-1933 (Chapel Hill: University of North Carolina Press, 1983).

5. Cf. Walter Dean Burnham, "Political Immunization and Political Confessionalism: The United States and Weimar Germany," Journal of Interdisciplinary History, 3 (1972) 1-30.

6. Michael H. Kater, The Nazi Party: A Social Profile of Members and Leaders, 1919--1945 (Cambridge, Mass.: Harvard University Press, 1983).

7. For a good summary, see on opposing sides of the issue, Tim Mason, "Intention and Explanation: A Current Controversy about the Interpretation of National Socialism," and Klaus Hildebrand, "Monokratie oder Polykratie? Hitlers Herrschaft und das Dritte Reich," in Gerhard Hirschfeld and Lothar Kettenacker, eds.,'Der Führerstaat': Mythos und Realität /The 'Führer State': Myth and Reality (Stuttgart: Klett-Cotta, 1981), 23-41, 73-97.

8. For argumentation along these lines see Hans Mommsen, "Die Realisierung des Utopischen: Die 'Endlösung der Judenfrage' im 'Dritten Reich'," Geschichte und Gesellschaft, 9 (1983) 381-420.

9. Martin Broszat, Der Staat Hitlers (Stuttgart: Deutsche Verlagsanstalt, 1969), now in English as The Hitler State (London and New York: Longman, 1981), John W. Hiden, trans. See also chapter 8, below, for fuller discussion and references.

1
The Collapse of Weimar

David Abraham

It would be correct to see in my account and interpretation of the later years of the Weimar Republic the
absence of a shared national project on the part of
German industry, or German capitalism more generally, as
a critical flaw, one which undermined both the social
and political foundations of the democratic republic.[1]
Indeed, that divergence of interests and of perceived
instrumentalities for accomplishing those interests,
affected not only industry, but also relations between
industry and what was at the time a very significant
rural sector. I would like in my remarks to return to
that complex of problems. For all the ways in which the
Weimar Republic was born under very inauspicious circumstances, and for all the various ways in which its first
several years seemed to cast doubt on its very ability
to survive, I think there is nevertheless much to be
gained by thinking of the Republic institutionally and
in its social composition and operation as a viable
bourgeois or liberal parliamentary republic. For such a
system to function for any length of time, it has to be
guided by, or it has to exist in the context of, a
shared national project, including some kind of elite
consensus on basic national goals and means for their
realization.

In addition to elite consensus, societies require
the fulfillment of two further conditions for stability,
conditions of equal import which should not go unmen-
tioned here. All democratic polities face the question
of popular consent. Elite consensus is not sufficient
for a polity, or even for elites themselves, if that
consensus is incapable of becoming a national project or
national consensus. That critical feature, popular
consent, is not something that elites can somehow mandate on their own. It must be elicited and won in
society and in politics. In Weimar it was not possible
simply to coerce the assent of some substantial portion
of the populace: unlike the Empire, Weimar was a real

parliamentary system with a rather advanced electoral system. In such a system, fraud and force could play only minimal roles. I have argued and would continue to argue that for several years, certainly for those years that we consider the Republic's more stable years (1924-1930), popular assent was provided basically by the Social Democratic Party and its affiliated trade unions. That cooperation was manifested both institutionally in labor's participation in a broad range of state mechanisms and arrangements, in the parliament through collaboration with the liberal parties, and in civil society as well as in the state. Yet, there was a serious problem, one brought about by the way in which the Social Democrats saw themselves. For years now, there has been a long debate about the nature and timing of the Social Democratic Party's transformation from class party to people's party. Whether that transformation started in 1875, with the Gotha Program, as some have argued, or as others would have it, really only in 1959, with the Bad Godesberg Program, or at some point in between, is an important matter. Either way, I think it is fair to say that during the Weimar period the Party was somewhere between a Klassenpartei and a Volkspartei but closer to being a workers' party. It was, for better or worse, a reformist but militant guardian of the daily interests of the organized working class.

What that means for this discussion is that the Party and the unions alike remained loyal to the proposition that their central social, economic, and political task was to obtain benefits for workers. Now, doing that would have been one thing if they had been able to define the national project, i.e., if labor had been in a position to make its project the project of the nation as a whole. That is something that social democracy after Godesberg, through the 1960s and 1970s, seemed to be able to do under the general rubric of growth through Keynesianism. In the Weimar period, however, it was not able to do that. Social democracy could, indeed, deliver or provide the popular support of a goodly portion of the working class for the democratic political and capitalist economic systems - although its readiness to compromise contributed at some points to the growth of a Communist opposition on its own left. But, be that as it may, such labor consent was costly precisely because the party still perceived itself as representing the interests of the workers. It pushed aggressively for workers' remunerative and social demands into 1930, and, in some respects, succeeded in protecting employed labor even in the Depression. Other social groups, especially the middle classes and business, certainly saw and resented what they took to be labor's undeserved and disproportionate success, and they rebelled against both labor and the political system that enabled labor to fare so well. Such pressures were too much for Weimar to withstand.

These pressures from labor played a part in the definition and redefinition of conflicts among German industrialists and between industrialists and agrarians. Among the issues that came to divide Germany's economic elites was the price to pay for popular assent, and the Social Democratic price remained high. This is not tantamount to blaming workers for Germany's economic crisis. Other factors, including dependency on American loan capital and the export economy (both of which were necessitated by various aspects of the Versailles settlement), were of greater importance. Yet I think it must be recognized that workers, organized through the Social Democratic Party and trade unions, refused, during the crisis, to give up the gains of the previous several years and to act like a model reserve army of the unemployed. That tenacity on the part of social democracy suggests the third element characteristic of any liberal democratic system, one that I would like now to put in the center light.

This third is a question as to the institutional capacity of a political system, i.e., its adequacy for organizing social negotiation between elites and citizenry. The institutional political capacity of the Weimar Republic, particularly that of its party system, proved inadequate for an assortment of reasons. Some were inherited from the Empire; some were consequences of the way in which the Republic was born; some, I would say, were simply generic to democratic republics as such. (And some, like the place of the military, are more difficult to locate.) The Weimar Republic simply did not enjoy the benefit of the institutional capacity necessary for the kinds of political shifts we have come to expect of parliamentary republics. We have witnessed, and in bad economic times we have come to expect, an electoral swing from a party like the Social Democratic Party, a party of popular legitimacy and economic redistribution in favor of the lower social orders, to a more conservative but loyally republican party representing the interests of private investment and capital accumulation. In other words, what happened during 1982 in West Germany (a swing from the SPD to the CDU) could not happen either in 1928 or in 1930. The institutional and electoral incapacity of the Weimar Republic was bound up with a number of factors not entirely generalizable to all political systems. It had to do, for example, with the way conservative parties in Germany were organized, with a support base in the (Protestant) countryside and a leadership drawn heavily from the eastern estate owners; it had to do with the existence of very well organized industrialists, who did not care to settle for less retrenchment of the welfare state when more was in sight; and it had to do with the fragmentation and lack of independence afflicting the "middle," bourgeois parties. The problems of the middle parties were especially severe, as has been demonstrated

most clearly in the work of L.E. Jones. These factors
combined led to a radicalized elite rebellion against
the consensus entered into in the mid-1920s, as well as
to the absence of a real "middle-class" alternative.

In my own work, I have tended, perhaps more than
others have, to separate the question of the Republic's
demise from the question of the Nazi victory. But there
is at least one sense in which they are of course inex-
tricable, namely that the Nazis helped to accomplish one
and were the beneficiaries of the other. Now, why the
Social Democrats were unable to expand beyond the boundaries of their working-class constituency (plus or
minus some other groups who supported them occasionally)
and make the kind of headway within the Mittelstand that
has been made since Bad Godesberg, is an important
issue, but one which I cannot address here. Why the
Nazi party proved to be the sole force capable of aggre-
gating not only the insecure and potentially authoritarian Mittelstand (in the classic portrayal of Eric
Fromm), but also many formerly liberal voters, remains
an important question (see the older work of Rudolf
Heberle as well as the new work by Thomas Childers and
Richard Hamilton). That the Nazi party was able to use
a distinct brand of authoritarian Populism to aggregate
various groups, who from 1919 or 1920 on deserted the
"liberal" middle-class parties, is indisputable. How
liberal those parties or voters really were is a tougher
question I cannot attempt to address here. But it is
indisputable that a very considerable portion of the
Mittelstand became politically homeless, abandoning the
bürgerliche parties, moving to and through several protest parties and movements, but not joining social
democracy. Ironically, the inability of social democracy to broaden its own base of popular support made it
harder for the national project of the elites, or even
for an elite consensus as such, to root itself in
society, particularly in the absence of popular
conservatism.

I think all of us at this table would have to agree
that whatever else it might have been about, Nazism was
about imperialism; it was about the conquest of Middle
Europe, quite independent of the question as to what was
to be done with the various populations living there and
markets available there. Such a program of imperialism
could, I have argued, appeal to all parts of the German
elite, rural, military, and industrial - whether
domestic-oriented and stagnant in the years 1925-1932 or
more dynamic and export-oriented. Indeed, along with
suppression of the labor movement and the restoration of
order, imperialism became, under the Nazis, something of
a "lowest common denominator" encompassing the various
and sometimes conflicting political and economic needs
and preferences of the divided economic elites. We also
know that there was a price to be paid: the elites lost

much of their autonomy and were exposed to considerable
uncertainty. As uncomfortable and troubling as this may
have been, most of the German elite was at least able to
pave its "road to serfdom" - with gold, mixed by the
Nazis with blood.

Before commenting on the relationship between business needs and the Nazis, I would like to return briefly
to the question of what factors prevented greater unity
among the pre-fascist industrial elites, greater unity
of either a conservative or social-liberal sort. Leaving aside today the agrarian elite and rural questions,
I would suggest, in extremely abbreviated form, that
there were primarily three problem-complexes, whose
problematic resolution impeded unity within the Weimar
capitalist elite. One was the question of the reinte-
gration of Germany into the western political and
economic systems, something referred to as Reparations-
politik (reparations policy) in the broadest sense.
Onerous or not, the Dawes and Young reparations plans
allowed some German industries to find the uses of
general adversity quite sweet. In other words, certain
kinds of industries could live with and even flourish
paying reparations while others seemed to be strangled
by them. The divergent positions adopted toward the
Young Plan by different industrial organizations and
politicians was but one symptom of this split. Another
very divisive key issue was Handelspolitik (commercial
policy) a very hotly debated and nasty issue within
German business organizations throughout the Weimar
years, especially after 1925. Over one-third of German
industrial production was exported, and, as I have shown
elsewhere, those exports were concentrated in a few key
industries, while many others were nearly totally dependent on the domestic market. Most-favored-nation trade
treaties threatened not just agriculture but also much
of cartelized heavy industry, which feared losing its
captive and high-priced home market. Commercial policy
was also a dangerous issue politically, for it provided
an arena for frequent cooperation with a consumer-
oriented social democracy, perhaps at the expense of
other kinds of businesses or businessmen. The third
problem area was provided by Sozialpolitik (social-
welfare policy) which ranked so high on the agenda of
German social democracy. As is still the case today,
different kinds of businesses and industries are affected to different degrees by wages and by social-welfare
costs. Some can afford it; some cannot. Wages as a
proportion of total costs are less burdensome to
capital-intensive industries than for artisanal industries and less burdensome, too, than is the case for
other industries where price competition is most
critical. Much the same held true for social costs
collected by the state through direct and indirect taxa-
tion (various forms of social insurance, for example).

Furthermore, labor made constant gains between 1925 and 1930, and German trade-union leaders were quite justified in proclaiming, as late as 1931, that German workers enjoyed the most extensive social-welfare in Europe, if not the world. Sozialpolitik had, in fact, become the virtual raison d'être for labor's politics. I think, without belaboring the point here, that the documentation is ample enough to demonstrate that such differences were very much on the minds of both German industrialists and German politicians. It is altogether clear that some German industrial associations were very upset with the stand taken on questions of Sozialpolitik by other industrial organizations and by sections of those bourgeois parties, for example of the Deutsche Volks Partei, which remained ready to compromise and compete with labor.

Wherever one draws the line between fractions or sectors of Weimar industry, one must, on the basis of the evidence, come to the conclusion that the virtual absence of vision, the difficulty in formulating a national project, which so plagued the industrial elite and reduced its political efficacy, was grounded in a conflicting diversity of economic interests. Real interests were at stake, and the sole apparently stable way to serve those interests - a Grand Coalition type of government with corporatist social and economic understandings embracing representatives of labor, capital, and the state - simply allowed the Social Democratic Party and trade unions too much influence. Particularly once the Depression cut off American capital and dealt such a severe blow to the export economy, the ability and willingness of German industry to gain popular legitimacy through cooperation with labor declined while the imperatives of capital accumulation became more pressing. And the balance of power within German industry shifted accordingly.

In pursuit of their fragmented interests, often riven in their organizations and needs, and now in opposition to a parliamentary democracy that divided them but allowed a laborist Social Democratic Party and its affiliated trade unions to tend to the interests of their followers relatively effectively even in a period of depression, leaders and representatives of agriculture and industry, especially mining and heavy industry, found themselves attracted to what the Nazis could offer. Especially after 1930, industrialists and agrarians found it increasingly difficult and undesirable to defend their varied and often conflicting interests within the framework and rules of the Republic. Nor did they any longer care to. The majority of them were clearly of authoritarian persuasion but unable to realize their own authoritarian schemes. The bürgerliche political parties both shrank and became increasingly rancorous and incompetent vehicles for the realization of capitalist interests, despite all the measures taken by industrialists to steer and reorganize them. The Brüning government was unable to break fully with the SPD, despite the Chancellor's severe, liberal-deflationary policies. The Papen regime, with its nearly total lack of popular support and strangling commitment to tariff protectionism at the expense even of Germany's export industries and commerce, and the Schleicher interlude, with its interventionist economic plans, political opening to the unions, and abandonment of estate agriculture, all disappointed, politically or economically, one or another or all fractions of German agriculture and industry.

After contributing decisively to undermining the Republic, German industrialists, agrarians, and their representatives found it necessary to attempt to harness the Nazi potential. The ultimate goal of the elites' offensive was the certainty that the state would culti-vate their economic needs and do so in a manner compre-hensive enough to incorporate their own divergent inter-ests. Yet, the political alternatives industrialists came to face were not directly of their own making, and the Nazi groundswell was something they had to face. Before 1933 there were probably not very many industri-alists who supported or followed the Nazis out of con-viction, even among the most socially reactionary Ruhr magnates. What is critical is that after a certain point, a different point for different individuals and groups of industrialists - some as early as Brüning, others as late as the appearance or failure of Schleicher's experiment - there was simply no acceptable and feasible alternative to the Nazis. A government of pure coercion, military or otherwise, was impossible; that is why the army refused to enforce a Papen regime and why Schleicher dickered with both the socialist trade unionists and the Nazi "left." A presidential dictatorship under the senescent Hindenburg could not last, and various anti-parliamentary, quasi-corporatist schemes (such as that of the League for Renewal of the Reich, which enjoyed substantial moral and financial support from industrialists) never got off the ground. No force other than the Nazis could claim real popular support, and support not limited to one class, while also demonstrating a commitment to eliminating Weimar's fragmented political democracy and generous social-welfare system. The German business elite wanted class peace, a "free" economy, and a reascendant Germany. Given the stubbornness, strength and commitment of so-cial democracy to the Republic, Germany's elites, in order to protect their social dominance, willingly ex-posed themselves to a potentially uncertain future under the Nazis. Just as Germany's industrialists, without any enthusiasm for the socialist movement or ideology, but in the absence of acceptable alternatives, collec-

8

tively compromised with the Socialists in 1918 in order to maintain the capitalist order, so by 1932 they were prepared to do the same with the Nazis.

In other words, to provide the briefest emendation of Professor Maier's opening characterization: the Weimar Republic faced three central problems very similar to those faced by other parliamentary systems - elite consensus, popular consent, and party-based institutionalization. Looking at any one of these questions in isolation is insufficient, and I have tried in written work and in discussion to show how those three problems interacted with each other and conditioned the ways in which each could develop.

NOTES

1. David Abraham, The Collapse of the Weimar Republic: Political Economy and Crisis (Princeton: Princeton University Press, 1981).

2
The Nazi Rise to Power:
A Comprehensible Catastrophe

William Sheridan Allen

My approach to the issues of the collapse of the
Weimar Republic and the rise of Nazism is likely to seem
very commonplace, perhaps even unsophisticated in its
stress upon known factors rather than overarching theories. But theory simplifies events in order to group
them, on the presumption that the crucial elements of
analysis can be extracted and then applied elsewhere,
hopefully with predictive reliability. Sometimes the
events themselves are so unique that this cannot work.
After fifty years of theoretical explanations of the
fall of Weimar and the rise of Nazism, using such varied
models as cultural determinism, societal atomization,
collective psychic trauma, or the mechanics of monopoly
capitalism, none of the theories that have been applied
has found general acceptance. Critics have shown so far
that each one is undercut by the data.[1] Moreover, the
simplification process often obscures essential mechanisms. Distant perspectives make distinct patterns
emerge more clearly, but to alter the perspective further, through the merging lens of theory, may distort
the details and mystify rather than clarify. What has
grown increasingly arcane from a distance becomes almost
banal in its comprehensibility from close up.
    Any unified theory may be particularly obfuscating
in the case of the rise of Nazism and the fall of Weimar
because, though they were coterminous in time, they were
causally separate and must be kept so in analysis if we
are to avoid confusion. Hitler and the Nazis exploited
the ills of the Republic (and helped intensify them),
but they did not create the Republic's problems nor were
they the only ones to profit from them. When the Weimar
system became moribund there were at least four potential replacements available: a communist dictatorship, a
military dictatorship, a restoration of the monarchy -
or its functional equivalent through continued presidential authoritarianism; and a Nazi dictatorship. Thus
the key question is why the latter prevailed over the

other options. But a revival of the Weimar Republic was
not among the realistic alternatives.

Nor should this be cause for heavy thinking. Given
the circumstances it faced, the wonder is not that
Weimar collapsed, but that it lasted as long as it did.
It had a bad beginning, the forces that created it
crippled themselves almost immediately, it was cursed
with a negative heritage, faced almost uniquely unpropi-
tious conditions, and had to confront all these problems
using a dysfunctional mechanism of governance within a
framework of endemic social stress. By its last years,
Weimar also had a vanishing consensus. The great majority of its citizens were casting protest votes for parties that were united only in their common condemnation
of the status quo.[2]

The birth of the Weimar Republic in revolution and
defeat gave the Republic permanent problems from the
start. A revolution that destroys the previous central
symbol of national cohesion inevitably brings everything
under question, including its own legitimacy. Any
government created at the moment of defeat is likely to
find itself associated with national humiliation, an
experience that Germany was subjected to by the victor
powers of World War I for five long years after the
armistice of 1918. A united revolutionary movement
might possibly have coped with these burdens, but of
course the Left in Germany split sharply before its
revolutionary gains were solidified. Not only was the
power of a coherent bloc thereby lost, to be replaced by
debilitating internecine conflict, but each wing of the
labor movement was further weakened through the loss of
the other's prime qualities (the rationalism of the SPD,
the activism of the KPD). At the time this was suc-
cinctly expressed in the saying that "the Communists are
all heart and the Socialists are all head," which
describes - in either case - a monstrosity.

Thus those who engendered the new state were not
only so busy fighting each other that they could not
sustain it, but even if both had wanted to defend the
Republic (and the Communists, of course, wanted the
opposite), they were also internally crippled to the
point where neither was likely to be able to do so.
From that point on, Weimar's continuance was tenuous.
It seems that what sustained the Republic more than
anything else was inertia, the incoherence of its enemies, and the occasional conversion of former non-
supporters such as Gustav Stresemann.

The lack of effective defenders for the Weimar
Republic might not have mattered had there been a strong
democratic tradition to fall back on, or if there had
been favorable conditions for the infancy of the new
republic. But the Second Reich's tradition of illiberalism, of anti-socialism, of anti-democratic values,
plus the heritage of Bismarck's successful cooption of

nationalism for the authoritarian cause, all worked
against the legitimization of Weimar. The inherited
elite leaders scorned parliamentary democracy. They
also refused to accept responsibility for their own
actions, which were generally selfish and short-sighted.
Worst of all, the "best" elements of German society gave
their moral support to right wing assassins, to military
desperadoes, and ultimately to the Nazis in their struggle against the Republic. So the customary societal
sanctions failed to curb extremism in pre-Nazi Germany.
It has also been argued that the German intellectual
community, for divergent reasons to be sure, gave
virtually no support to the Weimar state.[3]

Of course Weimar Germany's most indigestible heritage was that of the First World War, with its bequest
of violent attitudes and brutalized veterans. These
would have been hard for any society to reintegrate or
dissipate; in the case of Weimar, they were concentrated, reinforced, and deliberately harnessed to undercut
the regime. As for economic conditions, Weimar faced a
uniquely nasty series of events over the short span of
its existence: hyper-inflation, an automation crisis,
and the Great Depression. All undermined social and
political stability; even the so-called "prosperous" era
(1925-1929) was characterized by harsh deflation, structural unemployment, and an agricultural crisis of massive dimensions. Politically, these conditions heightened internal conflict and, more importantly, increased
disaffection from a regime that could not master them
(even though, to be logically consistent, a more appropriate response would have been closer cooperation, to
cope collectively with what were, after all, common
problems).

Instead, the economics of scarcity, when translated
into inter-group conflict, further intensified inherited
class divisions. Particularly, middle-class attitudes
in Weimar Germany were characterized by fear of status
degradation. To this there was added the dread of a
second, radical, proletarian revolution. The rigidity
of the prevailing social structure made such fears acute
and ultimately led many Germans to seek a non-threaten-
ing alternative to the class system itself - a quest
that Nazi demagoguery exploited through the slogan of a
"Volk community." Even before that hazy concept began
to be accepted, the destabilizing effects of social fear
were widespread.

Possibly these problems could have been confronted
rationally and systematically had the political system
functioned more effectively. But the division and ultimate collapse of the middle-class parties not only set
their erstwhile constituents adrift, the weakness of
these parties also helped preclude political problem-
solving. Part of the division in the middle class was
ideological. But part arose because Germany's bourgeoi

sie was united only in status defense. "Class representation" was not a practical reality because, as Larry E.
Jones has shown, there was no united middle class in
terms of common interests.[4] And finally, Weimar
Germany's dysfunctional system of proportional representation fostered weak leadership and the proliferation of
(largely ineffectual) parties.

All of these factors are well known and are repeated here not to rank order them but to emphasize that any
one of them would have severely stressed virtually any
governmental system. Their multiple interaction is the
key to the tenuousness of the Weimar experiment. In
combination they provide us with a more than adequate,
in fact a richly overdetermined, causation for the collapse of the Weimar Republic. Other theories may be
considered, but applying "Occam's Razor," we can conclude that an overriding theoretical explanation is
otiose. The Weimar Republic was assaulted by such a
conjunction of interrelated problems that it would have
required something close to a miracle to make it viable.
Its survival for a decade and a half, however halting,
is what needs explanation, not its ultimate demise.

A similar approach also proves to be the most useful one to analyze the rise of Nazism. By 1929, when
the Nazis began their spectacular rise to power, the
majority of Germany's voters were already alienated from
the Weimar Republic. Essentially, Hitler's party had no
effective opposition throughout most of Germany.[5]
There is even a sort of test for this point since, where
there was an intact and functioning political competitor
- the Catholic Center party - the Nazis made little
headway. Therefore, it was less some massive psychological predisposition to a charismatic Führer that fed
the Nazis their votes but, much more, the Nazi use of a
receptive pool of already alienated voters who lacked
effective representation for their (largely negative)
attitudes. What won these voters to Hitler was the
Nazis' uncompromising anti-republican and anti-socialist
propaganda plus some skillful tricks in delivering that
propaganda. Hitler's main contribution was to parlay
the mass backing thus obtained into political power.

There was no wizzardry in the process. This
bothers us, in view of the dreadful things that Hitler
later did. We would prefer an all-encompassing explanation so that we can use it to prevent some future would-
be Führer. But as Michael Marrus has pointed out in
another connection, big events (in the sense of terribly
significant, consequential ones) do not necessarily have
big causes. Secondly, in view of what happened later,
it behooves us to remember that Hitler did not promise
what he eventually would deliver: imperialism, terrorism, mass murder, and the destruction of Germany through
a reckless gamble for world power. We have to look at
what the Nazis did promise voters in the last years of

the Weimar Republic and, when we do, we find that their
message varied according to the group being addressed.
The only common threads were negative: attacks on the
Weimar system and particularly anti-"Marxism." Negativ-
ism was clearly the most effective approach for collect-
ing protest votes, and protest votes turned out to be
the largest pool available in the early 1930s.

Still, it is possible to identify particular groups
that were drawn to Nazism, as long as we exempt from our
generalizations that one-quarter of the country where
Catholic voters predominated. The total number of
German Catholics was closer to one-third, but if you
look at places where they predominated, the correct
figure is one-quarter. Elsewhere, the prime source of
the Nazi votes was the farm population, a large group at
that time: 30% of the population. Afflicted by a structural crisis that was intensified by the Depression,
farmers also found themselves abandoned by the traditional parties. Hence the Nazis wooed them with es-
pecial fervor. A second major constituency was the
small townsmen, threatened by modernization. We have
been so conditioned by the intervening demographic
shifts to think of big cities as the loci of "the
masses" that we might easily forget that the great
majority of Germans did not live in big towns in the
1920s. As Lawrence Stokes has pointed out, some 60% of
the German people resided in communities with fewer than
20,000 inhabitants, according to the 1925 census.[6] A
third major source of supporters can be identified less
by occupation or geographic location than by prior political behavior: the voters who had previously supported
the decaying middle-class parties, the short-lived
splinter parties, or those who had been non-voters. In
the sense of reflecting a general ideological stance
(fundamentally an anti-"Marxist" one), the Nazis became
what Jeremy Noakes has aptly called a Bürgerblock - a
bourgeois fusion ticket[7] (though, as Richard Hamilton
has demonstrated, it would be an error to see this purely in "class" rather than in ideological terms, since
the "middle-class parties" drew votes from across the
social spectrum, including many "tory workers"[8]).
Finally, the Nazis benefitted greatly from the novelty
of their movement (curiosity drew many Germans to Nazi
meetings) and from the "bandwagon effect" - at least
from 1929 to 1932 - by which latter date there were
clear signs that this was ebbing almost as rapidly as it
had previously flowed.

Still, the Nazis did build mass support among the
German electorate - 37% at their high point in July 1932
- and this was the fundamental lever that hoisted Hitler
into power. How did such a wicked and crazy movement
ever get that far? More precisely, how did Nazism man-
age to appeal to members of interest groups that were in
conflict, without alienating one group as fast as it

attracted its competitor? In short, what was the secret of the Nazi propaganda formula?

It seems to me that the essential point we need to focus on here is that the Nazi party was a movement of the skilled middle class. I know that the work of Michael Kater has shown that the Nazi membership encompassed much more than the middle class, though the middle class was always considerably overrepresented. But the leaders and functionaries of the party up to 1933 were overwhelmingly middle-class, particularly of the upper middle class.[9] In this sense it is fair to characterize Nazism as the first middle-class party with mass aspirations, and that is the key to understanding its effectiveness, especially in the organization and delivery of propaganda.

Ideologically the Nazis were committed to the goal of attaining power through the enlistment of support from all classes, across the entire country. Indeed, they were willing to subordinate virtually everything else, such as programmatic consistency, interest group coherence, or even human decency, to this goal. More importantly, they brought to their pursuit of this simple goal not just the resultant focused energy, but also the technical skills of the trained middle classes. The result was extraordinary efficiency.

From their middle-class background the Nazi leaders down to the local level already knew how to operate in the world of everyday business. They knew how to contract for the rental of halls or the leasing of equipment, how to get advertising designed and printed, how to do cost/benefit accounting for the running of a large scale organization. Their approach to practical problems was as hard-headed and realistic as their political philosophy was supercilious, wrong-headed and fuzzy. Only if we see the Nazis as calculating small businessmen turning their sharp skills to the task of winning votes for Hitler can we understand the effectiveness of their propaganda.[10]

A great example of this is the nexus between Nazi propaganda and self-financing. The frequently repeated but factually incorrect assertion that the Nazis were financed by heavy contributions from Big Business[11] is a particularly pernicious myth because it obscures the way in which the Nazis' need to find funding from their own voters led them to a more effective propaganda delivery system. According to Hitler's precepts, meetings with speakers constituted the best propaganda technique. That was a convenient theory, since for most of the Nazi rise to power it was also the only thing they could afford. At the local level, from 1925 on, all Nazi funds had to be self-generated. Far from supplying money for the point of contact with the voter, the higher offices of the Nazi party expected local units to contribute to them. What the party's higher offices did

do was organize and make available a broad selection of
speakers on a wide variety of themes and also supply
equally diverse printed propaganda - all to be paid for
in advance by local Nazi leaders.

Of necessity, therefore, local Nazi leaders learned
to adapt their choice of speakers, themes, and written
materials to the needs and interests of audiences in
their particular locality. Otherwise the message could
not be (literally) sold. Since Nazi ideology preached
contempt for human intelligence, the party had few problems being opportunistic about this. Whatever worked
was repeated; what did not was avoided. And since the
Nazis charged admission to their meetings and took up
collections at them, they had the simplest and most
easily measurable feedback system as to what worked with
their audiences: profit or loss from individual meetings. After 1929, when Nazi meetings began to show
strong profits, the surplus was reinvested into increasing numbers of meetings plus more written propaganda to
lure higher attendance at these meetings. The system,
in short, was self-feeding.

In the small towns and rural communities where the
Nazis were to get the bulk of their votes, the "entertainment value" of Nazi meetings was a major consideration. From a profit-making perspective, Nazi propaganda
activities can therefore be compared to religious revival meetings in the American Midwest at the same time.
But the major point to note is how the system was self-
financing, self-reinforcing, and self-adapting. If it
had not been clever propaganda it would have been sharp
business, but of course the point is that it was both.
Feedback and flexibility were the hallmarks, plus constant activism, as long as the process paid off.

Of course, none of this would have worked if a
constituency had been unavailable or if the content of
the propaganda had not been ideologically acceptable to
the audiences. As delivered to the German voter, Nazi
ideology in the period of the rise to power was the
familiar taken one step farther: patriotism, the need
for national unity, the promise of better leadership,
the rejection of the status quo, and the pledge to destroy "Marxism." The charismatic structure of Nazi
ideology (that is, its locus in Hitler as a person
rather than in a written doctrine)[12] was the key to
its combination of flexibility and cohesiveness. Its
extraordinary adaptation to locally varied concerns was
the work of the delivery system just described.

It was on the basis of these techniques and these
messages that Hitler's party was able to exploit the
favorable circumstances that arose after 1929: the collapse of the parliamentary system, the demise of the
middle class and splinter parties, the onset of the
Great Depression. In short, the Nazis were given a
brief opening and this permitted their propaganda tech

niques to work with a portion of the electorate, for a
while, and in some areas. As has been noted, they found
few supporters among the constituents of the Catholic
Center party. They also had little luck with the
"Marxist" voters, understandably, in view of their
anti-"Marxist" message. Among these Germans, "protest
votes" went to the Communist party, but stayed within
the "Marxist" political culture. From 1928 to November
1932 the net number of votes cast for the SPD and KPD
actually increased by some 810,000. And though the 37%
of the electorate that the Nazis got in free elections
is a sickeningly large figure, it is not a majority. It
was, however, enough.
    Which brings us to the final element in Nazi suc-
cess: luck. They were lucky in having their movement
sufficiently developed in time to exploit extra-
ordinarily favorable circumstances. They were lucky to
be hoisted into power at just the moment when their
techniques were playing out, when growing boredom and
indifference among their sometime supporters were
destroying the whole propaganda campaign. And above
all, they were lucky to find conservative leaders stupid
enough to entrust Hitler with power and to believe that
he could be used and controlled by them.
    There is obviously much more to be said about the
rise of Nazism, particularly about the mechanisms within
the party that permitted its insane program to become
dominant. Much also remains to be said about why so
many Germans were willing to vote at all for a party
whose basic indecency should have been evident from the
start. We also want to know more about why so many
Germans thought that casting protest votes was an effective political move. But I doubt that any overarching
theory will emerge to provide the key to these questions, any more than it has to explain the effectiveness
of Nazi campaign methods. Instead, the answers will
probably emerge from the mosaic of minor details, as
they were combined. The fundamental story of the rise
of Nazism is astonishingly commonplace, breathtakingly
banal: Hitler's party was in the right place, at the
right time, with the right forces to come to power.

NOTES

    1. Pierre Ayçoberry, The Nazi Question: An Essay
on the Interpretations of National Socialism (1922-1975)
(New York: Pantheon, 1981), provides an extensive, if
occasionally turgid, critique of most of the received
theories.

    2. Thomas Childers, The Nazi Voter: The Social
Foundations of Fascism in Germany, 1919-1933 (Chapel

Hill: University of North Carolina Press, 1983), 268.
In my view, most votes for the KPD and DNVP were
"protest votes" too.

3. While there is general agreement about the
negative attitude of right-wing intellectuals, there is
disagreement about the leftists. The case against them
is most fully stated by George L. Mosse's "Left-Wing
Intellectuals in the Weimar Republic" in his Germans and
Jews: The Right, the Left, and the Search for a "Third
Force" in Pre-Nazi Germany (New York: Fertig, 1970),
171-225, and by Gordon Craig, "Engagement and Neutrality
in Weimar Germany," Journal of Contemporary History 2
(April 1967): 49-63; counter arguments in Fritz K.
Ringer, "Mosse's Germans and Jews," Journal of Modern
History 44 (Sept. 1972): 392-97.

4. Larry Eugene Jones, "'The Dying Middle': Weimar
Germany and the Fragmentation of Bourgeois Politics,"
Central European History 5 (March 1972): 23-54. Further
specifics on the fragmentation of middle-class interests
are found in Heinrich August Winkler, Mittelstand,
Demokratie und Nationalsozialismus. Die politische
Entwicklung von Handwerk und Kleinhandel in der Weimarer
Republik (Cologne: Kiepenheuer & Witsch, 1972).

5. On this see Sebastian Haffner, The Meaning of
Hitler (Cambridge, Mass.: Harvard University Press,
1983), 52-62.

6. Lawrence D. Stokes, Kleinstadt und
Nationalsozialismus: Ausgewählte Dokumente zur
Geschichte von Eutin 1918-1945 (Neumünster: Wachholtz,
1984), 9.

7. Jeremy Noakes, The Nazi Party in Lower Saxony:
1921-1933 (Oxford: Clarendon Press, 1971), 249.

8. Richard F. Hamilton, Who Voted for Hitler?
(Princeton: Princeton University Press, 1982), passim.

9. Michael H. Kater, The Nazi Party: A Social
Profile of Members and Leaders, 1919-1945 (Cambridge,
Mass.: Harvard University Press, 1983), 184 and
following pages, and Table 10, 236.

10. This is further detailed on the basis of one
local operation in my revised edition of The Nazi
Seizure of Power: The Experience of a Single German
Town, 1922-1945 (New York: Franklin Watts, 1984), 75-84
and 143 and following pages.

11. See Henry A. Turner, Jr., "Big Business and
the Rise of Hitler," American Historical Review 75
(Oct., 1969): 56-70. See also Henry Ashby Turner, Jr.,

18

German Big Business and the Rise of Hitler (New York and Oxford: Oxford University Press, 1985).

12. Joseph Nyomarky, Charisma and Factionalism in the Nazi Party (Minneapolis: University of Minnesota Press, 1967).

3
Discussion

Participants addressed two basic sets of issues in the discussion. The first set was characterized by Charles Maier, who chaired the session, as "structural issues," those concerning the breakdown of the Weimar state and of various coalitions. The second set encompassed questions about who voted for the NSDAP and several possible influences on voting behavior. The responsibility borne by various social and economic groups for the events of 1929-1936 was a theme central to both sets of concerns.

A key question in the first group of concerns was whether the collapse of Weimar ought to be seen as a "crisis of the welfare state." Henry Turner argued in several remarks that the timing of the introduction of welfare policies and programs provided incentives for business and labor to adopt conflicting positions and eventually to bring the regime to crisis. Turner stated that Germany was the first state to develop extensive welfare provisions. As a result, German capitalists found that the burdens they bore compared unfavorably to those borne by capitalists in Britain, France, Belgium and America. At the same time, as evidenced by the SPD's rejection of Brüning's compromise offer in 1930, representatives of wage-earners could not persuade their constituency to accept the kind of back-down that labor is taking today. Germany, Turner argued, was "the cutting edge of the modern welfare state, and backing down was just something that the political exponents of the working class could not do."

Turner argued that this view of the collapse of Weimar suggests, in contrast to Abraham's argument, that it was not a failure of industrialists to unify their political interests and "impose their will" that accounts for the regime's demise.

David Abraham argued that the notion of a crisis in the welfare state implies that a point is reached beyond which accumulation as a priority must replace the redistribution carried out on behalf of the working class or of lower social orders generally. It implies, in other words, that at some point "the economy" can no longer afford redistributive measures. Abraham stated that this position, often advanced by critics of the welfare state, was similar to a Marxist view: the view that wage gains generate a squeeze on profits, which can then only be reversed through either the development of more capital-intensive production processes, or through capitalists' investment "strikes," or through the invocation of political mechanisms to discipline labor. Abraham argued that "just as Marx could never determine the 'socially necessary' minimum wage or immiseration threshold, so this theory cannot tell us what is the 'socially necessary' minimum profit level."

In any case, the difficulties of the SPD and of the Weimar welfare state were tied together. Given the politics the SPD had engaged in during the preceding years, Abraham argued, the SPD lacked a "positive" or "transformative" program. Its sole raison d'être was therefore the perpetuation of the welfare state, for which there is no "automatic stopping-point." Abraham stressed that whether one focused on the limits of the SPD, or accepted the whole notion that the collapse of Weimar could be seen as a crisis of the welfare state, the events of 1929-1936 were nevertheless usefully interpreted as the product of political behavior on the part of Germany's organized social forces.

Maier raised the issue of the regime's "revolutionary heritage," and attributed its weakness to a legitimacy that was "tainted" from its inception. Maier suggested that the intransigence of the SPD could be attributed to the presence of a strong Communist party on the left. The SPD leadership was forced to adopt a hard line, for the KPD threatened to garner the support of disenchanted workers.

Anson Rabinbach queried why the Social Democrats were "ghettoized" in terms of their support. And even given this situation, Rabinbach questioned what prevented a coalition from the side of those who may have seen the collapse coming.

Abraham cautioned that excessive blame should not be placed on the SPD. The SPD was not in a position to stage a revolution, so it left the government. The SPD could not have expected that its tactics would lead to the consequences that followed - decree rule, lasting parliamentary crisis, and the success of the Nazis - for the SPD had employed the same approach over the revocation of the eight-hour day in 1923. The explanation for the rise of Nazism would have to encompass, therefore, an account of why the government could not function after the SPD left.

* * *

The issue of the state's own needs was raised by Dan White. This approach which White attributed to Theda Skocpol, might serve to separate political decision-makers from business leaders. Maier echoed White's concern, and pointed out that if the collapse of Weimar is to be seen as a structural crisis, then the "milieu of decision-making" ought to be explored. Maier asked whether, or in what sense, there was a state in Weimar, and for whom it spoke.

Herbert Spiro underlined the role of the bureaucracy in German politics. Spiro stated that one finds in Germany a "continuing abhorrence of politics on either the French or British...models." Ordinary Germans with government-related problems would turn to the administration. rather than to their political representatives, Spiro said. In addition, Spiro argued that industry itself was organized on the model of the state, and that executives, with the possible exception of those at the very top, made their behavior conform to the example set in government ministries. Spiro stated that bureaucrats formed a greater percentage of the total population than in either Britain or France, and asked whether some more or less unified electoral behavior might be discerned. In assessing the role of bureaucrats in the collapse of Weimar and the rise of Hitler, Spiro asserted that bureaucrats could have, at the least, prevented the catastrophe.

*　*　*

Issues in the second set of concerns, voting behavior and influences on it, were addressed by Claudia Koonz. Koonz argued that the departure of Protestants from and loyalty of Catholics to traditional parties deserve explanation. Koonz stated that an explanation can be found by examining the role women played within religious organizations. Such an approach, according to Koonz, would entail a focus on the housewife as a "threatened occupational group," and an emphasis on the extent to which religious and social organizations were able to meet the social and economic crisis of the late 1920s and early 1930s. The implication was that the strength of female organizing in Catholic groups accounted for the loyalty that Catholic parties enjoyed.

To the criticism that women in Weimar Germany generally voted according to their husbands' wishes, Koonz offered several replies. Nazi vote among women mobilized much more slowly than among men, according to Koonz, and only came up to men's vote in 1932. Women in general voted more Catholic Center and less for the SPD than men, Koonz stated. Koonz added that research in this area is aided by the fact that men and women voted on different colored ballots in some districts.

Thomas Childers highlighted the continuity in the concerns and mentality of the middle class stretching back to before the First World War. Childers stated that there was a large constituency among the middle class that was satisfied with "traditional leadership."

Dieter Orloff emphasized the cumulation of crises - war, inflation, and depression - in explaining the way people voted. What was crucial in late Weimar was the widespread support among all sectors of the population for the NSDAP, a point Orloff thought to be supported by Richard Hamilton's Who Voted for Hitler (Princeton: Princeton University Press, 1982).

Thomas Childers attempted to integrate Richard Hamilton's findings on the voting behavior of upper and lower classes with the traditional view that the Nazi success was the product of lower middle-class support. Childers argued that party propaganda was directed to those who were traditionally seen as lower middle-class: small shop-keepers, white-collar employees, farmers and others. The party's appeals "emphasized their sense, if not their actual position, of economic anxiety." The NSDAP, according to Childers, appealed to "people who found themselves caught between big business and big labor."

Childers offered the criticism that the districts Hamilton employed in his study were not homogeneous with respect to income, and that studies such as Hamilton's are hampered by a lack of demographic data outside of Berlin and Hamburg. From the resulting educated guesses as to the social composition of various neighborhoods, all one can derive is a "rough indication" of income's relation to voting. Childers concurred with Hamilton that the appeal of the Nazis was indeed broader than previously believed. But Childers posed the query: to which elements of the various classes did the Nazis appeal? Here Childers recalled his own observation that political literature in Weimar "almost always" appealed to occupational groups. These groups were more than census categories, they structured how people thought about politics, Childers said.

Richard Hamilton answered that the appeals given by a party are not necessarily the same as the motives of its supporters, and that, in general, comparing motive and appeal is a complex subject. Hamilton argued that one set of evidence does not say anything definitive about the other.

Hamilton conceded that the districts in his study were not homogeneous. Hamilton stated that he had checked on twenty possible sources for data on smaller administrative divisions (precincts), but had not been able to locate the information. The use of local news-papers, the comparison of votes recorded in private clinics to those recorded in public hospitals, and the tabulation of votes in resort areas and ships at sea had

all supported his conclusions in the absence of more
precise demographic data. With the data available,
Hamilton said, one can not do any better than "educated
guesses," even on some key questions.

Hamilton stated that he was skeptical about the
importance and relevance of occupational groups to
political behavior: "intellectuals of every nation are
perforce required to make use of the statistical categories handed to them by the statistical office for who
knows what kind of bizarre reasons when first setting up
categories in the middle of the nineteenth century, but
they are ideas planted in people's consciousness, and
they take it from there." Hamilton argued that it was
the SPD which had implanted those notions, but
maintained that an analysis based on class or occupational groups was nevertheless ill-founded.

Hamilton's idea that occupational categories were
artifactual raised some objections. Childers reiterated
that the occupational categories were picked up by
"hard-nosed" politicians who used them in everyday
political campaigning. This, he argued, is a crucial
fact, even if motivations are indeed hard to ascertain.
Jane Caplan stated briefly that the occupational categories derived not from the mid-nineteenth century, but
from the language of the <u>Stand</u> (estate, order). Therefore, Caplan argued, those categories carried with them
an important history, one which may have had significant
consequences.

Freya von Moltke raised the issue of the timing of
the voting patterns observed by Hamilton, and stressed
that there were shifts in voting support over time.
Hamilton answered that, from May 1924 on, he found "the
same basic pattern from beginning to end."

Maier summarized Walter Dean Burnham's suggestion
in recent unpublished essays that in urban areas there
was a polarizing phenomenon: that is, the stronger the
working-class population, the larger was the Nazi vote,
for a vote for the Nazis was seen as the only effective
counterweight to the proletarian vote. This might account for the class correlation that Hamilton's findings
suggest, Maier said.

Childers concurred with the polarizing thesis and
went on to argue that the traditional view that workers
in heavy industry, mining and similar occupations were
bastions of support for Social Democracy and the KPD
(German Communist Party) is still valid. Workers in
small-scale manufacturing and handicrafts, Childers
said, constituted about forty percent of the population
and offered substantial support to the NSDAP.

Peter Hall offered a query that addressed both the
rise of Nazism and the fall of Weimar: were intrinsic
conflicts of interest - that is, social stresses - decisive, or was it the incapacity of social and political
institutions that shaped events? Hall argued, further

more, that Hamilton appears in his book to move from the
position that some classes were intrinsically open to
Nazi appeal by virtue of their underlying interests, to
a position that the NSDAP was simply better than other
parties at organizing all kinds of people for political
action. Hall cited Giovanni Sartori's distinction
between "the sociology of politics" and the "politics of
sociology" in this regard.[1] Hall went on to suggest
that the problem raised by Abraham's work - irreconcilable interests among two sectors of capital - forms a
part of this debate. One might ask, Hall said, if it
was not that interests were irreconcilable, but that
parliamentary and extra-parliamentary institutions did
not have the capacity to handle these conflicts.

NOTES

1. Giovanni Sartori, "From the Sociology of
Politics to Political Sociology," in Seymor M. Lipset,
ed., Politics and the Social Sciences (New York: Oxford
University Press, 1969), 65-100.

4
Nazism: Fascism
or Totalitarianism?

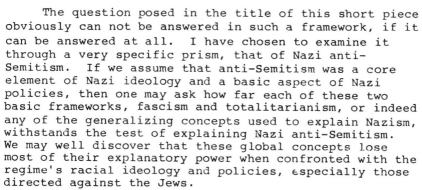

Saul Friedländer

The question posed in the title of this short piece obviously can not be answered in such a framework, if it can be answered at all. I have chosen to examine it through a very specific prism, that of Nazi anti-Semitism. If we assume that anti-Semitism was a core element of Nazi ideology and a basic aspect of Nazi policies, then one may ask how far each of these two basic frameworks, fascism and totalitarianism, or indeed any of the generalizing concepts used to explain Nazism, withstands the test of explaining Nazi anti-Semitism. We may well discover that these global concepts lose most of their explanatory power when confronted with the regime's racial ideology and policies, especially those directed against the Jews.

Of all the general interpretations of Nazism, that which places it in the comprehensive category of fascism remains, to this day, the most widely accepted.[1] The fascist interpretation appears in a Marxist version, as we shall see later, and in a non-Marxist version. In both cases, Nazi anti-Semitism, in its singularity and centrality, represents an important obstacle to this type of generalization. Most theoreticians of fascism resolve the problem by not taking account of anti-Semitism: their theories skirt the issue by avoiding practically any mention of anti-Semitism (save a few words, for form).[2] Others recognize the difficulty, but nevertheless search for a "common ground" among fascist movements, over and above what separates them.[3] Some historians have meanwhile attempted to integrate Nazi anti-Semitism into the framework of their general theory.

The inclusion of Nazi anti-Semitism in the framework of fascism theory can take three different forms: its reduction to a more fundamental ideological characteristic, its inclusion as a functional element in the particular dynamics of fascist parties, or its placement in a relation analogous to other, similar attitudes identified in most fascist regimes.

It was Ernst Nolte who, in his monumental study, Three Faces of Fascism, tried in the most systematic manner to reduce Hitler's anti-Semitism to an ideological characteristic common to all great fascist movements: anti-Bolshevism. For Nolte, the anti-Semitism of the Nazis was nothing more than a facet of anti-Bolshevism (the extreme form of anti-Bolshevism practiced by "radical fascists"):

> Hitler always succumbed to an ungovernable passion on the subject of bolshevism. He regarded it as the most radical form of Jewish genocide ever known - all his meager, pallid historical constructs culminate in this....However, according to Eckart's book [Der Bolschewismus von Moses bis Lenin. Zwiegespräch zwischen Adolf Hitler und mir, 1924], Hitler had specified another bolshevism ahead of Lenin's as an origin - that of Moses![4]

This identification of Judaism with Bolshevism permits Nolte to associate Nazi anti-Semitism with the anti-Bolshevism of other fascist movements; even though the texts Nolte cites give the distinct impression that it was anti-Semitism which determined anti-Bolshevism, more than the other way around. Moreover, the recent collection of Hitler's writings up to the drafting of Mein Kampf permit one to evaluate the relative importance of anti-Semitism and anti-Bolshevism: there are about three times as many references to Jews as there are passages dealing with Bolshevism, Communism and Marxism.[5] This reflects the evident difference between National Socialism and other "fascisms": in Nazism, anti-Semitism occupies a place that is both central and singular. It was the Jews and not the Marxists who were the target of Hitler's ideological declarations from beginning to end; the Soviet Union and even the European Communist parties were briefly Hitler's allies between 1939 and 1941; and the idea of a separate peace with Stalin surfaced again at the end of the war. Yet, any "pact" with the Jews was always unthinkable from Hitler's point of view. In the end, one can not be more explicit on the rapport between anti-Semitism and anti-Bolshevism than was Martin Bormann: National Socialist doctrine is totally anti-Jewish, which also implies anti-communist and anti-Christian. All these aspects are in National Socialism and all flow into the struggle against Judaism.[6]

According to the second mode of integrating anti-Semitism within the framework of fascism theory, racial anti-Semitism had existed in Germany since the end of the nineteenth century, but its passage from being a vague theory to becoming a political system required the structural conditions that are precisely those of fascist regimes. As Hans Mommsen has expressed it, it is

not enough to consider Nazi anti-Semitism as a more
radical variant of earlier trends. One must ask about
the structural conditions that transformed anti-Semitism
from mere propaganda into a savage radicalism.[7]

The following conditions (Mommsen illustrates them
through the structure of the NSDAP and of the Third
Reich) are, in his view, the typical structures of fascist parties and regimes: direct ties between the leader
and subordinate officials, ill-defined areas of responsibility, giving rise to a constant rivalry and internal
struggle which lead to a cumulative radicalization, the
moving force behind this being the constant effort of
each person to defend his ever-endangered position.[8]
Thus, the battle for the control of Jewish affairs would
have led to an increasing radicalization of initiatives
in that domain, and it is this which would account for
the final solution: it was a result of the internal
dynamic of a fascist party and regime.[9] We will return later to this interpretation of the events leading
to the final solution, but, from all the evidence, this
type of radicalization could not have maintained itself
against so many difficulties without the continuing action of a central force. Moreover, no comparable process can be found in the other fascist regimes.

Third, and a point on which it seems useless to
dwell, Nazi anti-Semitism has been compared to the
"racism" of Italian fascists toward Africans, Slavs
(Trieste, Fiume), and the Germans of southern Tyrolia;
the difference in degree, according to Wolfgang
Schieder, was only the effect of the war.[10] One must
ask why the war did not affect Italy in the same way,
and, more generally, how, in order to maintain at all
costs a theory of fascism, one can seriously entertain
such comparisons. In fact, as Karl Dietrich Bracher has
written:

> A general theory of fascism will always remain
> questionable when confronted with this problem
> [Nazi anti-Semitism and the extermination of the
> Jews]....While [Italian] fascism centered around
> the quest for the strong state, stato totalitario
> as the basis of a renewed impero Romano, Hitler's
> basic notion was the primary role of the race, the
> racist foundation of a future empire, to which the
> organization of a strong state was no more than
> instrumental - never an end in itself.[11]

In the Marxist conception of Nazism as fascism,
anti-Semitism is included in a manner even less coherent
than that of the liberal conception. The Marxist conception is, from the start, a piece of political propaganda camouflaged as history, it is a Soviet fabrication
of the 1960s on the side of the exterminators one finds
the Nazis as well as the Zionists, and, facing these

two, their victims, the Jewish masses. The objective of
the Nazis matters little; that of the Zionists is simple: to collaborate in the extermination of the majority
of Jews to insure that a minority will have the chance
to emmigrate to Palestine and to create a Jewish
state.[12]

At another level, the Marxist conception of fascism
tries to integrate systematically Nazi racism and even
the extermination of Jews in an orthodox, ideological
framework in which the final solution must be the result
of a deliberate policy of industrial and finance capital
to obtain enormous returns at little cost (slave exploitation of a work force always renewable according to
needs; the seizure of Jewish goods, etc.). Defended
notably by East-German historians,[13] this interpretation, as a whole, takes no account of the obvious: the
massacre of European Jews removed from the war industries a considerable work force. At the height of hos-
tilities, less than a quarter of the Jews in each convoy
escaped extermination upon arrival at the concentration
camps. According to the statistics, the final solution
represented for the German war economy a loss so large
that the goods derived from its victims could compensate
only an infinitesimal amount.[14]

Another Marxist thesis: the persecution of the Jews
was used by the Nazis and thus by big capital to divert
the attention of the masses from the crisis of the
capitalist system, from the absence of any true social
reform, etc.. Anti-Semitism therefore played the same
role in this circumstance as external aggression and the
war: the persecution as a necessary derivative. Here
again, the events do not agree with the theory. We
know, first of all, that the social change brought about
by Nazism was much more extensive than was often believed after the war.[15] We know further that public
opinion, during the 1930s, did not greet the persecution
of Jews with enthusiasm; Nazi anti-Semitism appeared to
tarnish the popularity of the regime.[16] And when it
came to the final stage, that of extermination, the
regime's anti-Semitic policies could not have served to
divert the attention of anyone, for those policies were
carried out in complete secrecy.[17]

Finally, for some West-European Marxist historians,
anti-Semitism does not belong at all in the interpretive
framework of the whole. The British historian T.W.
Mason, for example, revives a heterodox thesis on the
"autonomy of politics" within the framework of National
Socialism (autonomy necessary to lift the system out of
a crisis otherwise insurmountable). [18] Mason completely
dissociates the final solution from the rest of his
interpretation:

The SS was able, by virtue of its monopoly over the
information services and the machinery of terror,

of its position outside the legal framework, and lastly, by virtue of Himmler's special relationship with Hitler, to execute its ideologically determined task of the destruction of the Jews to the material detriment of the whole system. The way in which the political sphere emancipated itself from all reference to the needs of society is nowhere clearer than in the example of the SS, where the translation of ideology into practice was in flat contradiction to the interests of the war economy and yet was allowed to continue.[19]

Thus the overarching theory remains intact.

At the theoretical and methodological level, Reinhard Kühnl detaches Nazi anti-Semitism from the framework of orthodox Marxism: the discussion of these irrational elements requires new methods, and Kühnl suggests a recourse to psychological analysis joined with the analysis of society. He calls to mind Reich and Fromm: the key to the interpretation of anti-Semitism and the final solution does not lie at the level of social forces, but at that of the unconscious.[20]

Totalitarianism is the third major view with a generalized interpretation of Nazism.[21] On first sight, the anti-Semitic policies and even the final solution are better accounted for within this framework than within that of fascism, but only on first sight. The totalitarian interpretation of policies regarding the Jews generally draws on one or more of the following themes.

It is not, in the first place, a fundamental ideological motivation, so much as the desire for absolute domination over individuals and groups, which pushes the totalitarian system to crush them, and, when the voice of domination demands it. the absolute destruction of one group or another, indifferently. The enemy to be annihilated becomes a functional element in a system of absolute domination. One can imagine that, in order to terrorize the whole population or to galvanize its energy, first one group, then another, chosen arbitrarily, is the victim of persecution or total extermination.[22] According to the interpretation of Horkheimer and Adorno, the Jews were murdered at a moment when the fascist leaders could have replaced the anti-Semitic points of the program as easily as they might have moved teams of workers from one entirely rationalized factory to another.[23]

Secondly, the bureaucratic machine is the licensed instrument of power and of totalitarian terror. This machine is staffed by ordinary and interchangeable functionaries whose sole ambition is to fulfill their duties as well as possible. On matters concerning discrimination against a particular group, the machine, once under way, can progress from enforcing the most basic procedures of identification to total extermination. Numerous and diverse works confirm the central role of the totalitarian bureaucracy in the process of destruction: the monumental work of Raul Hilberg on the workings of the bureaucratic machine of destruction,[24] Hannah Arendt's polemic on Eichmann, the banal functionary of evil,[25] H.G. Adler's study of the deportation of Jews from Germany,[26] and the recent works by Christopher Browning on the role of Foreign Office officials in the working out of the final solution [27] and by Joseph Walk on anti-Semitic laws. [28]

The totalitarian interpretation of the extermination of the Jews comes up against several major difficulties, namely the centrality of anti-Semitic ideology among Nazi leaders and the non-functionality of the enemy in the National Socialist system.

It is useless to return to the motivation behind Hitler's own anti-Semitism; the same is true for Heinrich Himmler,[29] as well as for most of the elite of the NSDAP. As Karl Dietrich Bracher - himself an advocate of the totalitarian interpretation of Nazism - writes, through the theory and practice of mass extermination Nazi racial ideology became an end in itself.[30] If this is so, the totalitarian interpretation of the Nazi persecution of the Jews finds itself directly confronted with a major objection: the classical theory of totalitarianism, that which Hannah Arendt expounded in the early 1950s, postulates an ideological void at the core of the totalitarian system: the totalitarian elite does not believe in ideology; ideology is used only to delude and to galvanize the masses.[31] The Nazi system hardly meets this criterion. Furthermore, if the anti-Semitic ideology was a central motivation and priority of the Nazi elite, the persecution of the Jews must find its primary explanation outside of the constitutive elements of the totalitarian system: the totalitarian framework therefore explains only the method of destruction, not the reasons for it.

The centrality and autonomy of anti-Semitic ideology meant that, for the Nazis, the enemy was not interchangeable, and not replaceable according to needs. And contrary to a theory which assigns to the enemy the function of reinforcing totalitarian power and of permitting the massive use of terror against some in order to frighten and warn the others, the Jewish enemy was, in the final solution, exterminated in the greatest secrecy: a sacred end and not a means to other ends.

Thus, there does not seem to be an inclusive interpretation of National Socialism which can incorporate explanations of Nazi anti-Semitism and of the regime's anti-Semitic policies. Indeed, it is the reverse which seems to be true: Nazi anti-Semitism and the final solution throw into question global interpretations of Nazism.

NOTES

1. The concept itself is more and more contested, see especially Gilbert Allardyce, "What Fascism is Not: Thoughts on the Deflation of a Concept," American Historical Review 85 (April 1979): 367ff.

2. To see this, one need only peruse a recent work on theories of fascism, such as Wolfgang Wipperman's Faschismus-theorien (Darmstadt: Wissenschaftliche Buchgesellschaft, 1980).

3. Compare, for example, Stanley G. Payne, Fascism: Comparison and Definition (Madison: University of Wisconsin Press, 1980), especially 163, 195 and following.

4. Ernst Nolte, Three Faces of Fascism, Leila Vennewitz, trans. (London: Weidenfeld and Nicolson, 1965), 406. (Original title, Der Faschismus in seiner Epoche, 1963.)

5. Eberhard Jäckel, ed., Hitler. Sämtliche Aufzeichnungen 1905-1924 (Stuttgart: Deutsche Verlags-anstalt, 1980). The comparison was made possible by the detailed index accompanying the volume. The following key words were employed: (a) Bolschewisierung, Bolsche-wismus, Bolschewisten, Kommunismus, Kommunist, Kommunistische Arbeiter-Partei Deutschlands, Kommunistische Partei Deutschlands, Marxismus; (b) Anti-semitismus, Hebräer, Jude, Juden, Judenfrage, Judentum. By adding the term "Rasse" and its deriva-tives to category "b," one arrives at a ratio of refer-ences to Jews to references to Bolshevism around four to one. For the historian of the Nazi party, Dietrich Orlow, this irreducible centrality of anti-Semitism means that the Party's "ideology" reduces to the idea of the Aryan as absolute good and the Jew as absolute evil. Dietrich Orlow, The History of the Nazi Party 1919-1933 (Pittsburgh: University of Pittsburgh Press, 1969), 4 and 48.

6. Translated from Adolf Hitler, Libres Propos sur la Guerre et la paix, 2 vols. (Paris: Flammarion, 1954), 2:347.

7. Hans Mommsen in Totalitarismus und Faschismus. Eine wissenschaftliche Begriffskontroverse (Munich: Oldenbourg, 1980), 63-64.

8. Ibid., 24.

9. Hans Mommsen, "National-Socialism: Continuity and Change," in Walter Laqueur, ed., Fascism: A Reader's

Guide (London: Penguin, 1979), 178-9. We find here the "functionalist" conception of the Nazi system transferred to the theory of fascism. This functionalist conception will be discussed below. Hans Mommsen and Martin Broszat, among others, have become its most important exponents since the end of the 1960s.

10. Wolfgang Schieder in Totalitarismus und Faschismus, 58.

11. Karl Dietrich Bracher, "The Role of Hitler: Perspectives of Interpretation," in Laqueur, ed., Fascism, 201-2.

12. On this subject see Lucy S. Dawidowicz, The Holocaust and the Historians, 68ff.; and Erich Goldhagen, "Der Holocaust in der Sowjetischen Propaganda und Geschichtsschreibung," Vierteljahrshefte für Zeitgeschichte, vol. 28, no. 4 (1980): 502ff., especially 504.

13. Konrad Kweit, "Historians of the German Democratic Republic on Anti-Semitism and Persecution," Leo Baeck Institute Yearbook, vol. 21 (London: Secker & Warburg, 1976), 174.

14. Raul Hilberg, The Destruction of the European Jews (Chicago: Quadrangle, 1961), 645ff.

15. See especially David Schoenbaum, Hitler's Social Revolution: Class and Status in Nazi Germany 1933-1939 (Garden City: Doubleday, 1966).

16. Compare Ian Kershaw, "The Persecution of the Jews and German Popular Opinion in the Third Reich," Leo Baeck Institute Yearbook 26 (1981).

17. The thesis according to which the persecution of the Jews was a way of diverting the attention of the masses from the problems of the regime or from those of the capitalist system could be presented in a more elaborate manner than this resume; but the argumentation is essentially the same. See, especially, Abraham Leon, La Conception matérialiste de la Question juive, nouvelle édition (Paris: Études et documentation internationales, 1968), 155.

18. For the various versions of this theory as applied to Nazism, see in particular Pierre Ayçoberry, La Question nazie. Les interprétations du national-socialisme 1922-1975 (Paris: Ed. du Seuil, 1979), 93ff. and 233ff.

19. T.W. Mason, "The Primacy of Politics - Politics and Economics in National-Socialist Germany," in S.J. Woolf, ed., The Nature of Fascism (London: Weidenfeld & Nicholson, 1968), 192.

20. Reinhard Kühnl, "Probleme einer Theorie über den deutschen Faschismus," Jahrbuch des Instituts für deutsche Geschichte (Tel Aviv: Universität Tel-Aviv, 1974), 3:322ff.

21. "Fascism" and "totalitarianism" are not necessarily opposite concepts: Italian fascism was proclaimed to be totalitarian from the beginning. Contemporary analysis, however, tends to oppose the two concepts: in essence, fascism implies the centrality of an ideology (anti-Marxism), while totalitarianism suggests a system of domination that could achieve a rapprochement with a regime that would appear to be its ideological opposite (Nazi Germany and Soviet Russia, for example).

22. The arbitrary choice of the enemy to be terrorized would be one of the fundamental characteristics of the totalitarian system. See Carl Joachim Friedrich and Zbigniew Brzezinski, Totalitarian Dictatorship and Autocracy (Cambridge, Mass.: Harvard University Press, 1956), 10.

23. See Max Horkheimer and Theodor W. Adorno, "Eléments de l'Antisémitisme," in La Dialectique de la Raison. Fragments philosophiques (Paris: Gallimard, 1974), 214.

24. Hilberg, The Destruction of the European Jews.

25. Hannah Arendt, Eichmann in Jerusalem: A Report on the Banality of Evil (New York: Viking, 1963).

26. H.G. Adler, Der Verwaltete Mensch. Studien zur Deportation der Juden aus Deutschland (Tübingen: J.C.B. Mohr, 1974).

27. Christopher R. Browning, The Final Solution and the German Foreign Office (New York: Holmes & Meier Publishers, 1978).

28. Joseph Walk, ed., Das Sonderrecht für die Juden im NS-Staat. Eine Sammlung der gesetzlichen Massnahmen und Richtlinien - Inhalt und Bedeutung (Heidelberg: C.F. Müller Verlag, 1981). Nearly two thousand anti-Semitic ordinances and decrees were issued in twelve years for the territory of the Reich alone. The last known decree, dated February 16, 1945, stipulated:

"When it is impossible to remove the records dealing with anti-Jewish activities, they must be destroyed to prevent their falling into enemy hands." _Ibid._, 406.

29. On this subject, see Josef Ackermann, _Heinrich Himmler als Ideologe_ (Göttingen: Musterschmidt, 1970).

30. Karl Dietrich Bracher, _Die Deutsche Diktatur. Entstehung, Struktur, Folgen des Nationalsozialismus_ (Cologne: Kiepenheuer & Witsch, 1969), 464.

31. Hannah Arendt, _The Origins of Totalitarianism_ (New York: Meridian Books, 1958).

5
Comments on Reactionary Modernist Components of Nazi Ideology

Jeffrey Herf

Karl Dietrich Bracher has written that the fundamental problem of the interpretation of National Socialism is the underestimation of the importance of Hitler
and of Nazi ideology by his political contemporaries.
Bracher goes on to add that even with the benefit of
hindsight, subsequent scholarship has often repeated
this error. In these brief comments, I will argue
first, that for different reasons, both Marxists and
modernization theorists have contributed to this underestimation, and second, that there has been a rethinking
of the problem of National Socialism and modernity in
the last decade which helps us to account both for the
origins of Nazi ideology before 1933 and for its persistence after the seizure of power; and third that if we
think again about the mixture of modernist and anti-
modernist elements in Nazi ideology - in particular, the
way it reconciled irrationalism and a fascination for
modern technology - we gain some insight into how it was
that totalitarianism in power did not succumb to the
demands of capitalist, technocratic or even nationalist
rationality, but rather pushed ideological absolutes to
their grim conclusions.
Hitler's ideology was the decisive political fact
of the Nazi regime up to the catastrophic end. Very few
of Hitler's conservative allies and left-wing opponents
expected this would be the case. Some argued that
Hitler was the cynical opportunist that would abandon
principle for the sake of power, or that he was a tool
of the capitalists who would do him in as soon as he had
done the dirty work of smashing the unions and parliamentary barriers to rearmament. And still others, at
the time and since, argued that National Socialism was
fundamentally a complete rejection of the modern world
and its values. As such, its ideological dynamism would
be broken apart in the course of actually governing and
administering the most advanced industrial society in
Europe. Why this did not happen has been the focus of a
scholarly debate ever since.

Historians of Nazi ideology have stressed that it was the product of a cultural-political revolt against modern industrial society and an attempt to recapture the purer virtues of a mythic, preindustrial Gemeinschaft. How then did German nationalism, and subsequently National Socialism, become reconciled to modern technology? Barrington Moore Jr. drew the reasonable conclusion that "the basic limitation" of this "Catonist" rural imagery lay in its uncompromising hostility to industrialism as a result of which it would develop into rural nostalgia. Ralf Dahrendorf and David Schoenbaum further developed the idea that Nazi ideology was incompatible with industrial society. Dahrendorf argued that despite their anti-modernist ideology, the demands of totalitarian power made the Nazis radical innovators. The "strong push to modernity" was National Socialism's decisive feature resulting in a striking conflict between Nazi ideology and practice. The "veil of ideology should not deceive us," for the gap between ideology and practice was so striking that "one is almost tempted to believe that the ideology was simply an effort to mislead people deliberately." Along similar lines, Schoenbaum described National Socialism as a "double revolution," that is, an ideological war against bourgeois and industrial society waged with bourgeois and industrial means. In his view, the conflict between the anti-industrial outlook of the Nazi ideologues and the modernizing practice of the Nazi regime was resolved through an "inevitable rapprochement" between the Nazi mass movement and the state and industrial elites which that movement had promised to destroy. In Schoenbaum's view, the Nazis made their peace with modern technology because it was needed to carry out their anti-modernist politics, but not because they could discern any intrinsic value in it.

The problem is that in too many very important instances, Hitler's practice coincided with his ideology. If ideology and practice were so at odds, how do we account for their terrifying unity during the war and the Holocaust? The thesis of a "double revolution" suggests ideological cynicism where ideological consistency and belief existed. The "strong push to modernity" or at least to certain aspects of modern society existed, but not at the expense of Nazi ideology. The main problem with this approach has been its neglect of the modern aspects of Nazi ideology. Marxists have had little difficulty in this regard because they have examined the Hitler regime as one variant of fascism which, in turn, was a form of capitalism. At times, such analyses suggested that Hitler was merely a tool of the capitalists or that Nazi ideology actually declined in importance after the seizure of power. And at their best, such as Franz Neumann's classic Behemoth, they employ a utilitarian concept of class and ideology which rules out the

possibility that the Hitler regime could act against the
interests of German capital - as indeed it did when it
pursued radical utopia and genocide above all else.   The
route is different, but the conclusion the same for
Marxists and modernization theorists: whether it was due
to the anti-modernist nature of the ideology or the
overwhelming power of class interests, both suggest that
Nazi ideology could not explain the actions of the
Hitler regime.   They are thus at a loss for explanations
of the triumph of ideology in the Third Reich.

The first observer of National Socialism to grasp
clearly the intertwining of modernist and romantic aspects was neither a historian or social scientist.   In
1945, Thomas Mann wrote that "the really characteristic
and dangerous aspect of National Socialism was its mixture of robust modernity and an affirmative stance
towards progress combined with dreams of the past: [it
was] a highly technological romanticism."   Walter
Benjamin had hinted at such a thesis in his post-war
essays on Ernst Juenger while Max Horkheimer and Theodor
Adorno developed the idea of the intertwining of reason
and myth in the Dialectic of Englightenment. The superiority of Mann's formulation over that of the critical
theorists is the unflinching instance on pointing to the
link between Germany and National Socialism rather than,
as Horkheimer and Adorno did, generalizing Germany's
particular misery into a malaise of modern civilization.
The irony of the critical theorists was that they were
often perceptive but for the wrong reasons.   It simply
was not true that, as they put it, "the fully enlight-
ened world" radiated disaster triumphant.   The idea that
Germany suffered from too much Enlightenment strains the
historical record beyond recognition.

In the last decade, a number of historians, social
theorists, and literary critics have suggested fruitful
avenues of investigation for reconsidering the connections between modernist and anti-modernist elements in
Nazi ideology: Karl-Heinz Bohrer, Joachim Fest, Tim
Mason, Eike Hennig, Charles Maier, Moishe Postone, Karl-
Heinz Ludwig, Anson Rabinbach and Klaus Theweleit come
to mind.   It seems that history and social science have
now caught up with Mann's literary insight.   Based on a
study of the work of major figures of Weimar's conservative revolution - Ernst Jünger, Oswald Spengler, Hans
Freyer, Carl Schmitt, Werner Sombart, and Martin
Heidegger;   lectures and essays produced by German engineers and professors of engineering at the technical
universities from the turn of the century up through
1933; and of writings from the Nazi Party before 1933
and propaganda of the Nazi regime after the seizure of
power, I have described an ideological tradition I call
reactionary modernism.

My argument is the following: Before and after the
Nazi seizure of power, an important current within Ger-

man nationalist ideology entailed reconciliations between antimodernist, romantic and irrationalist ideas
with the most obvious manifestation of means-ends rationality, modern technology. The thinkers I am calling
reactionary modernists never described themselves in
precisely these terms. But this tradition consisted of
a coherent and meaningful set of metaphors, familiar
words, and emotionally-laden expressions which had the
effect of converting technology from a component of
alien, Western Zivilisation - reason, intellect, inter-
nationalism, finance, materialism, liberalism, the
Jews - into an organic part of German Kultur - community, form, blood, will, productivity and, finally, race.
The reactionary modernists combined political reaction
with technological advance. Where German conservatives
had spoken of technology or culture, the reactionary
modernists taught the German Right to speak of technology and culture.

Reactionary modernism was not primarily a pragmatic
or tactical orientation, which is not to deny that it
transformed military-industrial necessities into national virtues. Rather it incorporated modern technology
into the cultural system of German nationalism without
diminishing the latter's romantic and anti-rational aspects. By reconciling technology and Innerlichkeit, the
reactionary modernists contributed to the Nazification
of German engineering, and to the primacy of Nazi ideology and politics over pragmatic calculation of the national interest up through the end of the German dictatorship. They were contributors to the unity - rather
than the separation - of totalitarian ideology and political practice in the Hitler regime.

In short, after the seizure of power, the ideol-
ogue did not give way to the technocrats, Albert Speer's
account notwithstanding. German war production was in-
ferior in both quantitative and qualitative dimensions
compared to that of the Allies. Declining enrollments
in the technical universities, lack of understanding of
the relation between research and technological advance
were legacies of the attack on rationality which the
reactionary modernist tradition sustained, despite its
embrace of technology. Time does not allow presentation
of the hundreds of descriptions of tanks filled with the
German soul or Fritz Todt's odes to his landschaftsver-
bundene Strassen - highways bound to the landscape.
But the master administrator of cultural traditions in
the Third Reich, Joseph Goebbels, offered a succinct
view of what I am describing. In 1939, addressing the
Berlin Auto Show, standing between a Volkswagen on one
side, Hitler on the other, Goebbels noted that some
feared that

technology will make men soulless. National Socialism never rejected or struggled against technology. Rather, one of its main tasks was to fill
in inwardly with soul, to discipline it and to
place it in the service of our people and their
cultural level. National Socialist propaganda used
to refer to the steel-like romanticism of our century. Today this phrase has attained its full
meaning. We live in an age that is both romantic
and steel-like, that has not lost its depth of
feeling. On the contrary, it has discovered a new
romanticism in the results of modern inventions and
technology. While bourgeois reaction was alien to
technology, if not filled with ignorance and hostility to it, and while modern skeptics believed
that the deepest roots of the collapse of European
culture lay in it, National Socialism understood
how to take the soulless framework of technology
and fill it with the rhythm and hot impulses of
our time.[1]

As this passage indicates, Nazi ideology was by no
means an unambiguous rejection of modernity. Its embrace and rejection of aspects of modernity was highly
selective. The Nazis could rearm Germany but they inherited a sufficiently healthy dose of political irrationality so that they were incapable of winning a war
against any but the most defenseless of their enemies.
The primacy of politics of the war years rested on ideological foundations evident in Nazi ideology before
1933.

NOTE

1.   Deutsche-Technik (March 1939): 105-6.

6
The New Nazi Rulers:
Who Were They?

Michael H. Kater

In order to determine who the new Nazi rulers were,
especially after 1933, it is necessary to characterize
the common Nazi party membership. This can be done best
in terms of social class. In the Nazi membership from
1919 to 1939, what I call the elite class (former aris-
tocracy and upper middle class) was overrepresented, the
lower middle class was also overrepresented, and the
working or lower class was underrepresented (more about
this in my book with Harvard University Press, The Nazi
Party: A Social Profile of Members and Leaders, 1919-
1945).[1] Within the Nazi leadership in approximately
the same time period, counting various cadres from
Blockleiters to Gauleiters and Reichsleiters, the elite
class was also overrepresented, but more heavily so than
in the case of the common membership, the lower middle
class was again, overrepresented (in this case, about
equal to the degree of overrepresentation in the common
membership), and the workers were more heavily under-
represented than in the membership.
        Hence, at least one preliminary observation may be
made. In terms of class representation, the Nazi functionary corps rises above the common membership: the
leaders tended to come from an upper-class (or elite-
class) backround much more frequently than did the common members. Conversely, the workers were less frequent
in the hierarchy. This puts in serious doubt the theory
of social marginality that has been upheld for years,
after the classic statement made by Daniel Lerner in his
book, The Nazi Elite (Stanford: 1951). One may go further and say that the Nazi leaders appear to have been
characterized by the same criteria of social selection
as the governing elites of other (modern) state systems.
        The hypothesis that Nazi leaders were more akin to
conventional, western leaders of modern times is further
strengthened by the following sets of correlation:

> - positive correlation between Nazi leaders'
>   operational function (usually expressed in
>   rank) and class,

- positive correlation between Nazi leaders'
  rank and training and/or experience
- positive correlation between Nazi leaders'
  job security (job tenure in civilian life)
  and rank,
- positive correlation between Nazi leaders'
  age and rank,
- positive correlation between Nazi leaders'
  age and class.

The picture thus far is to be qualified after taking into consideration the development after 1933, the
year of Hitler's coming to power. At this time, the
Nazi leadership was called upon to govern and administer
within the inherited state system, short of engineering
a quick "revolution." It now turned out that despite
the high relative degree of (formal) elite-class affinity, the Nazi leadership cadres' high relative and absolute strength of lower-middle-class elements in their
midst precluded "rational" governance, which may ideally
be viewed as a consequence of elite-class traditions.
Lower-middle-class predominance in the Nazi hierarchy
after 1933 meant the continuation of a value system
specifically linked to (German) lower-middle-class mentality (identifiable, in an ideal-typical sense, with
Stammtischkultur). The most significant indication of
the prevalence of what one might call sub-elite-class
principles of governance in the Nazi hierarchy after
1933 was the existence of Menschenführung as a precept
of administration. For Menschenführung belongs to a
meta-emotional category that is anathema to reason (or
the rationality which modern governments demand); it is
grounded in Herzensbildung (among other notions militat-
ing against intellect) and manifests itself through
Schulung (a specifically National Socialist vehicle of
training).
Schulung, Herzensbildung, Menschenführung as hallmarks of anti-rational administration are all espoused
by the Old Fighters, the Nazi functionaries who joined
the NSDAP before 1933. This is solidly documented by
the source material. Hence it seems clear that the Old
Fighters were the principal champions of the distinctive
lower-middle-class value system which marked the
administration of the Nazis.
A difficulty arises after the discovery that Old-
Fighter status correlates positively with rank, age,
class, job security in civilian life, training (formal
education) and/or experience, at least in the setting of
the Nazi leadership. These correlations associate Old
Fighters not with sub-elite-class elements but, on the
contrary, with elite-class ones. How is this to be
explained?
There is something inherently paradoxical about the
Nazi leadership corps: it is characterized at one and

the same time by rational (elite-class) and irrational
(specifically lower-middle-class) marks of distinction.
This makes it so utterly complex a phenomenon. As the
regime progressed, the recruitment pattern seemed to
bolster the irrational and inefficient: closure at the
upper ends of the hierarchy prevented young, traditionally educated members of the elite class to enter the
cadres in order to fill leadership positions. Instead,
they wandered off to industry or, more important, the
Wehrmacht. The increased use, by the Nazi leaders, of
arbitrary power also points in the direction of the
irrational, if it is assumed that arbitrary power is
generally not wielded by rationally governed state systems. On the other hand, vestiges of rationality, of
efficiency, are observable in pockets of the leadership
such as the SS, the Organisation Todt, the Health
Generalkommissariat Dr. Karl Brandt, the Ministerium
Speer, and others. Until 1945, the Janus-faced character of the Nazi regime persisted, and this raises, once
again, the old questions about modernity versus tradi-
tionalism, technology versus artisanal processes, tech-
nocracy versus quasi-feudal governance, urbanity versus
provincialism.

NOTE

1. The book was published shortly after this paper
was submitted. The Nazi Party: A Social Profile of
Members and Leaders, 1919-1945 (Cambridge, Mass.:
Harvard University Press, 1983).

7
Discussion

The discussion which followed presentations by Saul Friedländer, Jeffrey Herf and Michael Kater focused on two main issues: the social background and beliefs of the Nazi leadership, and on the role of Nazi ideology in the regime.

Peter Jelavich, addressing the first of these two issues, challenged the paradox that Michael Kater had established between the elite social background of Nazi leaders and their "lower middle class mentality." Jelavich asked whether there was, for example, an "elite mentality" to which elites were being untrue when they espoused lower middle class beliefs. Jelavich argued that what Kater observes is not a class-specific mentality after all. Elites can "spout rubbish," Jelavich noted; that behavior is not unique to the lower middle class.

Hans Mommsen suggested that a consideration of the character of Nazi leaders should include not only those leaders who stayed with the regime up to the end, but also include those who left before 1933 and those who stayed "but had the attitude that they could not change things, and therefore, in a way, were partly in opposition to what was going on." Mommsen said that another factor should be added to the discussion: namely, the fact that Nazi Germany was a society that lacked a means of preventing corruption among its elite. This self-serving tendency was reinforced by the large measure of non-communication among top leaders. Mommsen noted that a "petty-bourgeois mentality" papered over the internal corruption and crimes of the regime.

On the question of officials leaving or staying on with the regime, Kater rejoined that those who remained were "technocrats fascinated by charisma," to form what Kater termed a "lethal combination." Stanley Hoffmann interjected that simple ambition, rather than "romantic seduction," may account for the behavior of technocrats and other officials.

Joseph Rovan stated that few of the top and middle-ranking Nazi leaders came from the leading families in Weimar. Moreover, Rovan argued, the bare fact that the people Kater mentioned belonged to one class or another is not enough to explain their beliefs: what is significant is that their "personal destinies" had been of "professional or personal marginality." Drawing on his own study of SS officers in Dachau, Rovan argued that in the background of Nazi leaders "something has broken in their personal destiny."

Jane Caplan also addressed the issue of the leadership in the SS, citing Gunnar Boehnert's characterization of them as an educated elite.[1] Caplan suggested that background studies on all of the various leadership groups, SS, SA and others, are necessary for an understanding of Nazi leaders in general.

Kater noted that he had worked on leadership in the SS previous to his current book, and that he was aware of and in agreement with Boehnert's study.

Richard Hamilton asked Kater to spell out what percentage the lower class, middle class and elites constituted among the population as a whole, in view of Kater's claims that elites and the lower middle class were over-represented in the party and its leadership and that the lower class was under-represented. Kater cited figures from his book that the elite constituted 2.78% of the working population, the lower middle class constituted 42.65%, and that the lower class constituted the remaining 54.56%.[2] Hamilton suggested that the larger groups ought to be divided, and emphasized the need for precision in a discussion of over- or under-representation of classes.

Hamilton also echoed Jelavich's point on whether there was actually a paradox to be found between belief and background among Nazi leaders. "Why not just take it straight?" Hamilton asked. As a final point, Hamilton noted that there is no study of the mentality of the 15 million people under discussion, not even in the work of Ralf Dahrendorf or of Hans Geiger.[3] "Is mentality class-specific? I believe it is," but until there is hard evidence, "we have to hang up a question mark," Hamilton concluded.

On the question of whether there is class-specific mentality, Kater said that one must deal always with "mixed types," and that the particular background of one person or another is not crucial, because the groups under consideration are quite large.

Juan Linz first commented that one should compare the social background of the Nazi leadership not to society as a whole, but to the leadership of other contemporary political parties. One may find a fundamental difference between the Nazis and conservative and bourgeois parties, Linz said. Second, Linz cautioned that there may be a difference between elites that were a

part of the party before it attained power and those
that joined afterwards. Every party that is in power is
likely to attract elites, Linz argued, one has to be
careful in making judgments about the class background
of members once the party has become the only access to
power. Third, Linz commented that Nazi ideology was
multi-faceted; it appealed to different sectors of the
population with different aspects of the whole. Nazi
ideology was consciously or unconsciously available to
many people. Fourth and finally, Linz noted that education is a problematic measure of class status in Weimar,
as German society was a society in which many people
pretended to a certain level of education and reading;
this was not particular to a particular social class,
but to mass politics.

Kater responded to Linz that comparison with repre-
sentational patterns in other parties would indeed have
been ideal, but that there are no data for those other
parties, except for some material on the KPD and the
SPD. On the question of the old versus the new elite,
Kater answered that one is faced with "blurred lines,"
but that he attempted to draw them as accurately as
possible in his book. Kater noted lastly that Linz's
point on education was well taken, but that one is
forced to draw up ideal types while keeping in mind
"margins of error."

On questions of ideology, such as those raised in
Herf's presentation, Hans Mommsen registered skepticism
about the use of ideology in explaining Nazi history, as
"it is very difficult to define what makes the Nazi
ideology a distinct one." Mommsen suggested that a
return to a consideration of structure would help an
understanding of the regime. On the Nuremburg Laws, for
example, Mommsen said, anti-Semitism was a "playground
for the party," for it was the only function not taken
up by government ministries.

Mommsen further remarked that he was critical of
Eberhard Jäckel's interpretation of ideology, and that
Hitler's ideology was not related to concrete programs.
Mommsen agreed with the interpretation of Martin Broszat
that a negative selection among the top leaders took
place. Mommsen noted that anti-Semitism was a "weak
point" where "cumulative radicalization" could take
place. By way of conclusion, and also bringing in a
consideration of Hitler to an understanding of his ideology, Mommsen suggested that Hitler should be considered as a man who lived with a mentality that was far
removed from actual, political reality.[4]

Joseph Rovan said of Nazi ideology that "things are
not elaborated at the beginning, but they came readily
to life." What was given to ordinary party members and
even to high-ranking members was not the real ideology,
until close to the end of the regime. This "second
ideology," domination for the sake of domination itself,

became evident to Germans only in Himmler's last speeches, Rovan said.

Herf responded that Hitler's ideology was not hidden, for it was revealed as early as Mein Kampf. This, for Herf, brought to mind the issue that Karl Dietrich Bracher had raised: why was this ideological statement not taken seriously? Herf suggested that one reason for this was the apparent contradiction between modern and traditional elements.

Several participants in the discussion considered the notion of the "reactionary modernism" in Nazi ideology, as Herf had presented it in his paper. Thomas Childers said that Nazi ideology was not anti-modern, but that there was a clear reaction by the party to the social ramifications of industrial modernization.

Dietrich Orlow argued that the combination of reaction and modernism was not unique to Nazi ideology. No modern society is without a reactionary element, Orlow said, "the two things always go together." Orlow offered an example from the United States, citing a "marvelous slogan" used by Pepperidge Farm in its advertising campaigns: "fully automatic equipment guarantees grandmother's old-fashioned taste." What was peculiar about Nazism, Orlow said, was that its negative images were always personified:

> whatever is against what the Nazis are proclaiming is identified with people....It is not that you are against an issue, you are against or for a particular type of person. And it is that which seems to me to be more unique than modernization combined with nostalgia.

Charles Maier suggested that one had to consider the nature of the pre-modern values included in Nazi ideology. Maier noted that the traditional values appealed to by the Nazis were often those involving death, conflict and irrationality: "they are not quite the same as grandmother's warm kitchen smells."

On this question of whether reactionary modernism was specific to Germany, Jeffrey Herf rejoined that in no other country, with the possible exception of Japan, were the contrasting elements as "starkly" positioned.

Anson Rabinbach commented that, by 1936, "people who could not cope with serious production processes were being phased out" of government service. The replacement of such individuals as Krämer [Minister of Economics, 1933-34] was an attempt to get völkisch ideologues out of government service, Rabinbach argued. As part of the rearmament program, Rabinbach said, they were replaced by solid technocrats whose völkisch ideals were mere overlay. Rabinbach finally suggested that ideology served quite a different purpose from that of integrating reaction and modernity. Ideology, according

to Rabinbach, played a role in institutions and in professional life. Ideology served as a test of allegiance
to the regime, and also gave individuals a sense of
purpose. What remains to be explored, Rabinbach said,
was the impact on mass consciousness of this enormous
production of ideology.

Herf responded that the purpose of ideology, simply
put, is that it "makes sense of the world."

Mary Nolan queried how far down the ranks of civil
servants an ideology of reactionary modernism actually
penetrated. Herf answered that in the course of his
research, he had read the material that engineers read,
such as professional and trade journals, but that he had
not perused material that engineers had themselves written. Just how far down reactionary modernism penetrated
has to be inferred, Herf commented. Franz Neumann, Herf
noted, had predicted that technicians and engineers
would be the first to react against Hitler. But this
did not come to pass, Herf said, adding that he had been
led by this observation to explore the notion of reactionary modernism. If the perception that Germany could
not technically win the war had predominated at the
time, Herf said, then one would say that reactionary
modernism did not enjoy wide currency.

Dan White commented that one cannot speak simply of
Nazi ideology or Hitler's charisma once the regime is in
place, for from that point on, Hitler was, in Max
Weber's terminology, the legitimate authority. Moreover, White said, the ideology did have a certain
"crazy" rationality, but a rationality nonetheless: from
certain premises about society, policies followed.
Germans believed that this was legitimate and right.
White noted that one ought to bear in mind recent and
contemporary manifestations of similar processes, such
as the wide-spread sterilization of Blacks in the American South and the apartheid and Bantustan policies of
South Africa. White argued that "we may say that the
whole policy was lunatic, but I don't think we should do
it in such a way that we fail to see why people were
doing what they were doing in the circumstance....I
don't think we should see people responding in some kind
of mad, crazy way....People lived in routine ways and
operated because they thought it was okay."

Saul Friedländer's comment that Nazism was the
relation to Hitler, prompted David Kaiser to ask Friedländer to separate the role of ideology and that of
Hitler himself. Charles Maier also queried in what way
Friedländer considered Hitler to be central. Friedländer rejoined that many Germans thought and said that
Nazi ideology was "trash," but no one said that Hitler
was trash.

On the balance between modernity and anti-
modernity, discussion Chair Stanley Hofimann commented
that there can simply be two "domains," a "means-ends

rationality at work," which nonetheless allows room for
ideology "as compensation." "I'm not sure that one
needs to produce a synthesis" of "soul" and "daily
task," Hoffmann said. Hoffmann concluded with a remark
on what was new and unique about the Nazi regime: the
connections between ideology, the state, and the leader.
In the Nazi regime there was both a state ideology and a
charismatic leader who had authored that ideology
(unlike, say, Stalin) and who defined the purpose and
orientation of the state bureaucracy. The state bureaucracy functioned according both to the logic of ordinary
rationality and according to the illogic of the ideology
and dictates of the Führer.

NOTES

1. Gunnar Boehnert, "The Jurists in the
SS-Führerkorps, 1925-1939," in Gerhard Hirschfeld and
Lothar Kettenacker, eds., Der"Führerstaat": Mythos und
Realität (Stuttgart: Klett-Cotta, 1981), 361-374.

2. Michael Kater, The Nazi Party: A Social Profile
of Members and Leaders, 1919-1945 (Cambridge, Mass.:
Harvard University Press, 1983).

3. Ralf Dahrendorf, Society and Democracy in
Germany (Garden City, N.Y.: Anchor Books, 1969,
copyright in 1967); Hans Geiger, Die soziale Schichtung
des deutschen Volkes (Stuttgart: Ferdinand Enke Verlag,
1932).

4. Anson Rabinbach offered the example of policies
on which Hitler was uncompromising, such as the shipping
of marble for Städtebau. Saul Friedländer commented
later that one can employ a function analysis in some
areas, but not in those with which Hitler was obsessed,
and that anti-Semitism was the core of his obsession.

8
Politics and Polyocracy:
Notes on a Debate

Jane Caplan

These remarks will be ruthlessly eclectic. They are not intended as an exhaustive review of the long debate about the nature of National Socialist rule, but as a framework for discussion at this conference.[1]

First, a reminder of two early and still fertile sources for the view of the Nazi state as polycratic. Franz Neumann, in his work Behemoth (1942), proposed that Nazi Germany was controlled by four co-equal power groups: big business, the army, the Nazi party, and the bureaucracy. He argued that "the state" had become a competitive arena, that it lacked a true sovereign, and that therefore the Nazi system could not be regarded as having a state in the sense understood in political theory. Ten years later, Hannah Arendt analyzed the Nazi state in chapter 12 of The Origins of Totalitarianism (1951). She saw it as promising stability in order to disguise its permanent instability in practice. It was dominated by a movement, and was thus structureless, because a movement has only direction, not structure. Politically, it spawned a multiplicity of offices, in order to create confusion about the true location of power. The sociopolitical atomization of the masses was paralleled and completed in the amorphousness of the entire political system, including its top leadership. Crucially, Arendt saw this system (or anti-system) as something planned and intentional, though she seems less clear about who was the agent of the planning (usually Hitler, but not always). It was this note of intention and planning that was caught in the elaboration of totalitarianism theory, which became increasingly unhistorical (as well as polemical and reductionist) as it was developed in the 1950s. This was the principal analytical tool available to non-Marxist historians when they started work on the archival materials that became abundantly available from the 1950s.

Neumann's work, however, acted as a kind of bridge back to the earlier ideas. Indeed, the political analysis underlying his general conclusions in Behemoth had tended to make them less assimilable to the more rampant growths of totalitarianism theory than was Arendt's metaphysics. To different degrees, the simplicities of totalitarianism theory were questioned by historians such as Broszat, Mommsen, Peterson (even Bracher) and others, as the evidence accumulated on how the Nazi political system actually functioned, what its political components were, and so on. The idea that someone or something in the Third Reich exercised an effective "monopoly of control" began to look increasingly implausible. A series of new insights began to arise, partly because old questions had been investigated through the use of new evidence. Two crucial gains, for example, were new ideas about the relationship between the structure of the Nazi regime and the structure and motivation of the pre-1933 NSDAP and Broszat's core thesis about the relationship between the regime's structure and the generation and execution of its policies.[2]

To see where we stand now, let us consider what questions these more recent polycratic interpretations have addressed, and what they have not and perhaps can not answer. First, they offer an explanation of how the Nazi regime was stabilized in 1933: by a mutually exploitative parasitism (or perhaps epiphytic system would be more appropriate) of the new leadership with the existing elites and institutions. This lends historical depth to the propositions about a mixed power structure, by elucidating the precise process by which the several components were brought into their uneasy political relationship. The very amorphousness of the new state, along with the sophistication of the bureaucracy, helps to explain the absence of any effective resistance after the mid-1930s. Mommsen's concept of parasitism suggests an explanation of the direction in which the Third Reich was heading - the exhaustion of its own bases of support - and lends shape to the battles in the 1940s between Bormann and Himmler over the sources for its potential restabilization.[3] Broszat's concept of "trialism" ascribes to Hitler a role and a sphere of action set in the real context of policy and its execution, rather than leaving him in the fictitious world of his own absolute plenitude to which he obviously aspired.[4]

These are only the most recent (and perhaps most contentious) conclusions yielded by research which has repudiated the never very secure idea of the totalitarian monolith. It seems to me, however, that as this depth of vision has been attained, so also the field of explanation has tended to shrink. We are left with a richly differentiated account of the functioning of the Third Reich as a political system, but only as a political system. Its relationship to the social formation as a whole, and more specifically to class structure, has been relatively ignored, despite a few notable efforts

such as Broszat's 1970 article.[5] Even the limited
agenda proposed by Hüttenberger - to examine the structure of relations between ruling groups and parts of the
population - is still largely unresolved (though he has
made some steps towards this in his recent work[6]). In
that sense, though we are further ahead than Arendt, we
are still behind Neumann.

How can further progress be made in building the
political analysis of the Nazi state and power structure
onto an analysis of the social formation which it dominated? This is obviously a question that can be ap-
proached both empirically and theoretically. Empirically, one reason for which we do not have much sense of
the relationship between the state and civil society in
Nazi Germany is that we do not know very much about the
history of that society, or have not up until now.
This, too, is changing, for example with the publication
of the volumes Bayern in der NS-Zeit, of Ian Kershaw's
work on Hitler and popular opinion, and of more informal
accounts of social relations under National Socialism.[7] Such accounts of the effectiveness of the state
in relation to its own citizens are the necessary counterparts to analyses of the way in which policy was for-
mulated and executed at the level of leadership. As far
as the further investigation of the state itself is concerned, it will be helpful when more work can be done on
the social composition and status of the civil service
and the new bureaucracies. Another issue that needs
more discussion is the time-frame within which the Nazi
period should be studied. The political dividing-line
of 1933 has less and less canonical status left to it,
but 1945 has been less challenged until recently. Of
course, there is no point in repudiating conventional
boundaries just for the sake of it, but I think it has
to be recognized by historians that the concept of the
"Year Zero" is simply a convenience, and needs to be re-
interpreted in social and political history.

It is easy enough to run off a list of empirical
research projects which could use and develop the insights of research into the history of the Nazi state.
It is more difficult to say what theoretical lines
should be followed, if any, and historians are bound to
have sharp disagreements on this. My own view is that
one cannot ask many questions about how societies are
ruled, and how national political agendas are set and
executed, unless one has some concept of the state and
of its relation to civil society. These concepts need
to be clearly articulated, and not left as silent part-
ners in the work of historical explanation. A concept
of class, and of class relations, is also axiomatic.
Given this, there are two basic ways of approaching theoretical issues. One is to continue to investigate the
relationship between particular classes, and the personnel and policies of the Nazi regime, in terms of both

representation itself, and to consider the extent to
which the Nazi regime did or did not function to maintain the state as a mechanism to prevent the antagonisms
derived from the economic relations of production from
consuming the classes and the society itself.[8] This
is only a more abstract formulation of the self-destruc-
tiveness of National Socialism which Mommsen has
argued.[9]

The utility of such approaches will no doubt be
contested by many because of the apparently polemical
implications. Perhaps less controversial is the idea of
pursuing Neumann's line of investigation into the nature
of Nazi political rule, as an issue in political theory.
There is a large and fascinating literature on this,
both from the 1920s and 1930s, and in current writing.[10] Though the clash of neo-Hegelians and neo-
Kantians may have been drowned by the louder noise of
street fighting towards the end of the Republic, the
corruption of a major tradition of German intellectual
thought is surely not an inherently marginal subject.

Finally, a few words about the so-called intention-
alism/functionalism debate. On a minor point, this
conference will have fulfilled an urgent desire of mine
if it can agree to put into circulation an alternative
to "functionalist," which already has a recognized and
inapplicable meaning. (Unfortunately, it did not: my
candidate would be "structuralist.") But more seriously, behind the facade of charge and counter-charge of
"trivialization" in recent historiography, there is an
important debate about the principles and nature of political responsibility and political morality in states
and societies characterized, as contemporary ones are,
by an extreme division of labor. If we want lessons
from history, and perhaps see Nazi Germany as peculiarly
fitted for yielding them, then this is among the most
urgent of them. Mason's article for the Führerstaat
volume contended that "the crucial problem for National
Socialist politics was to destroy as many enemies as
possible while going down fighting to the bitter
end."[11] From the perspective of 1983, that sounds
like an all too familiar strategy.

NOTES

1. For a longer summary, see Peter Hüttenberger,
"Nationalsozialistische Polykratie," Geschichte und
Gesellschaft, vol. 2 (1976): 417-42.

2. For the first, see Hans Mommsen, "National
Socialism: Continuity and Change," in Walter Laqueur,
ed., Fascism. A Reader's Guide (Harmondsworth: Penguin,

1979), 151-92. For the second, Martin Broszat, The Hitler State (London and New York: Longman, 1981).

3. Hans Mommsen, Beamtentum im Dritten Reich (Stuttgart: Deutsche Verlagsanstalt, 1966), chapter one.

4. See the articles by Mommsen, Mason and Ian Kershaw in Gerhard Hirschfeld and Lothar Kettenacker, eds., Der "Führerstaat": Mythos und Realität (Stuttgart: Klett-Cotta, 1981); also Ian Kershaw, Popular Opinion and Political Dissent in the Third Reich (Oxford: Clarendon, 1983).

5. Martin Broszat, "Soziale Motivation und Führerbindung des Nationalsozialismus," Vierteljahrshefte für Zeitgeschichte, vol. 18, no. 4 (1970): 392-409.

6. See his article on pressure groups in Hirschfeld and Kettenacker, eds., Der "Führerstaat."

7. Martin Broszat et al., eds., Bayern in der NS-Zeit, 4 vols. (Munich: Oldenbourg, 1977-81); Ian Kershaw, Der Hitler-Mythos (Stuttgart: Deutsche Verlagsanstalt, 1980); "informal" studies include for example Jochen Köhler, Klettern in der Grossstadt. Geschichte vom Überleben 1933-1945 (Berlin: Wagenbach, 1981), and similar oral histories, or Detlev Peukert and Jürgen Reulecke, eds., Die Reihen fast geschlossen. Beiträge zur Geschichte des Alltags unterm Nationalsozialismus (Wuppertal: Hammer, 1981).

8. See Nicos Poulantzas, Classes in Contemporary Capitalism (London: NLB, 1975).

9. In, for example, his contribution to Hirschfeld and Kettenacker, eds., Der "Führerstaat."

10. For example, Dietrich Kirschenmann, "Gesetz" im Staatsrecht und in der Staatsrechtslehre des Nationalsozialismus (Berlin: Duncker und Humblot, 1970); Bernd Rüthers, Die unbegrenzte Auslegung: Zum Wandel der Privatrechtsordnung im Nationalsozialismus (Frankfurt/Main: Mohr, 1968); Michael Stolleis, Gemeinwohlformeln im nationalsozialistischen Recht (Berlin: Schweitzer, 1974); Joseph Bendersky, Carl Schmitt, Theorist for the Reich (Princeton: Princeton University Press, 1983).

11. In Hirschfeld and Kettenacker, eds., Der "Führerstaat," 40.

9
Traditional Elites and National Socialist Leadership

Michael Geyer

I.

In judging the role of army, industry, and bureaucracy in the Third Reich, the Nuremberg tribunal's answer to the juridical and ultimately moral question of responsibility set the tone for the subsequent debate on the Third Reich. If many ruled, then many shared responsibility for the deeds of the regime. If only Hitler ruled, then at best the "many" contributed to Hitler's rise or, possibly, profited from it. If it could be shown that they did not even contribute to the rise of Hitler, then Hitler and the National Socialist movement had to shoulder the blame on their own. They became phenomena sui generis - unconnected to anyone before, after, or around them.[1] They could be acknowledged as historical facts, by traditional elites and historians alike, with a combination of puzzlement and horror.

The question of responsibility is studded with problems. Even after working through the layers of affirmation, explanation, puzzlement, distortion, and apologia that have accumulated since 1933, it remains difficult to pin down the precise role of military, industrial, and civil service leaders or of whole institutional complexes. Leading officers successfully misrepresented their role in operational planning for war and in preparing for the campaign against the Soviet Union in particular, to mention only two cases.[2] For a long time, industrialists sidestepped the issue of forced labor during the war and bureaucrats conveniently forgot about the many Nazi-sympathizers in their own ranks. With some effort and a great deal of empirical work, these and similar misrepresentations can be corrected - only to discover that the issue of the responsibility of traditional elites looms even larger after plowing through the factual evidence.

What should one study to analyze the role of traditional elites in the rise of Nazism and in the consoli-

dation of National Socialist rule? Most commonly it is
suggested that one study the relations of these elites
and their institutions to Hitler and the Nazi leadership, possibly even to the movement at large.[3] This
approach assumes that the links between Nazi leadership
and traditional elites can best be understood by looking
at the encounters and interactions between them or at
the general statements of one about the other. While we
learn a great deal about interactions between various
groups, public and private institutions, as well as individuals, we comprehend little about what motivate them
and we do not understand the context of these interactions. We get a very pointillistic picture of institutions and even individuals, but we learn next to nothing about their main activities and their raison d'être,
except if we assume that it consisted in negotiating
with each other. This assumption is nonsensical, and
yet industrialists and top managers seem to have exhaus-
ted their daily schedule in writing opinionated letters
about general politics; the military institution seems
to have done little else besides fending off or contain-
ing the Nazis; moreover, it seems that predilections and
ideological commitments of some officers governed the
military's connection to the Nazi leadership.
Many historians use this pointillistic approach.
Thus, we know a great deal about economic policies and
politics, but we know next to nothing about managerial
decisions concerning production, markets, and prices.
If we survey the literature on the various state bureaucracies, we wonder whether they did anything at all.
Until recently we also knew remarkably little about what
the military did between 1930 and 1938 except that it
was engaged in a series of encounters with Nazi organizations, Nazi ideology, and, ultimately, Hitler. No
wonder that resistance was discovered everywhere from
1933 on. Only when some historians realized that the
military leadership had to run an army and had to organize rearmament, and that both did not come easily and
automatically, did interpretations begin to change.
Cast in the light of running the military, much of what
previously had been described as resistance became part
and parcel of intra-service rivalries, bureaucratic
politics, or even petty jealousies.[4] By the same
token, many links between Nazis and traditional elites
which were not formally set down and negotiated - as,
for example, a partial identity of goals or outlooks[5]
- suddenly became apparent. The shift in what we study
has changed our evaluation of the role of the military
in the Third Reich, and one might expect the same for
industry and bureaucracy, if similar methods were
applied.
This shift is less innocent than it appears. Many
argue that the process of rearmament or, for that matter, of management decisions, is not at all important

for understanding the actions of traditional elites and
their relation to the National Socialist leadership.
Rather, rearmament reflected the long standing pursuit
of a German Machtstaat.[6] What shaped the German army
and its relations to the National Socialist regime in
the 1930s is not what the armed forces actually did, but
where the army came from. The resulting argument shows
a premodern Prussian elite that survived World War I and
the revolution in 1918 unscathed, and escaped the cage
of the Weimar Republic as soon as the republican forces
weakened. While some argue that these "traditional
elites" (which are not just elites that have remained
dominant for a long time, but who have otherwise adapted
and changed, but are truly premodern or "feudal" forces)
survived very well into the 1940s with their restorative
and untimely pursuits, others would more likely argue
that either the traditional elements were whittled away
one by one or that a slow transformation in favor of
National Socialism took place from within. In this view
power is invested in the military by tradition, rather
than gained and maintained. It comes with the status of
the officer corps which, in turn, is defined by an un-
changing Prussian outlook. (A less charitable interpretation of this approach would point to the reification
of originally polemical or even historical categories
which are made into historical actors or causes that
take on their own lives independent of actors and
events.) Historians who study the rise of Hitler[7] would
violently oppose a view that attributes so much power
and influence to traditional elites and tends to interpret the Nazi movement and Hitler as a mere successor
and its politics as a mere intensification of previous
(Wilhelmine) movements and politics. Yet, despite all
differences, these historians share in many ways the
same approach. For just as the study of the German military does not necessarily lead to a study of how and to
what end the military organizes violence (and a study of
German industry to a study of production), a study of
Hitler does not necessarily lead to analysis of how and
to what end authority and legitimacy in the Third Reich
were gained. As far as Hitler is concerned, most historians are interested in finding out what he has said
and written. They interpret what he did in that light.
Obviously, it is very interesting to see whether or not
Hitler's actions conformed to his previous writings,
just as it is enlightening to know that the military's
choices and decisions are not that novel, but fit a well
established pattern. (Both might be questioned, but
that is not the point.) It matters, though, that politics and policies shrink to a discussion of visions and
outlooks which, more often than not, transcend history,
be it by reference to a proverbial premodern outlook of
the German traditional elites or to the scripts of

Hitler that reveal what is described as irrational radicalism and dogmatism. Both lie conveniently beyond the actual history of the Third Reich or for that matter, any history, for they were mythical constructs from the very beginning.[8]

The shift of focus from the actual process of the organization of violence with its many tensions and obstacles, to the process of gaining and maintaining authority and legitimacy[9], or, for that matter, to the reconstruction of production, recasts the question of responsibility and gives the issue of traditional elites in the Third Reich, once again, a sense of political action and political process, a sense of conflict and choice. Naturally, traditions played a role in this process, just as fanaticism had its place. However, they were bound into concrete political processes and into the material and ideological context of the 1930s, in which traditions as well as fanaticism had to be practiced. Only the actual organization of violence showed how important and how successful traditions were at shaping the business of the military institution and only political practice indicated how important and effective fanaticism was in influencing society and in running the Nazi state.

II.

Rearmament was a key process in defining the interplay among the military, industry, and the National Socialist leadership. For all three, rearmament became a central focus of their respective activities; it contained tremendous advantages as well as liabilities for them; and while all considered rearmament as important or even vital for the future of the Third Reich, they did not consider it a goal in itself. In each case, it was a prerequisite for further action. Whether or not these further actions could be taken depended to a large degree on the shifting configuration of the three forces in the armament process itself. In this way, rearmament decided over the options for the future.

Rearmament also ruled out a return to the past, for the decision to rearm was one of the main sources for the collapse of the domestic compromises over distribution in the Weimar Republic, and it subsequently broke apart the last vestiges of an international order that was already seriously jeopardized by the dissolution of the international monetary order and the general turn to protectionism. Rearmament, however, did not automatically bring together the military, National Socialists, and industry. In fact, one of the reasons for the longevity of the presidential regimes between 1930 and 1933 was the unwillingness and the inability of these groups to find a compromise over rearmament and to come to an understanding on who would control it.

The control of rearmament was at the core of the
negotiations between the military and the National Socialist leadership over the participation of the National Socialist rank and file in military preparations and
exercises. It also figured prominently in the exchanges
between President Hindenburg and Hitler over the potential participation of the latter in a new coalition government. A prospective deal was enticing for all participants, but trade-offs were very difficult to negoti-
ate. The military leadership was most interested in the
paramilitary rank and file which offered a way to regain
a solid base in society, lost in the troubled years
between 1917 and 1923 and never recouped. The National
Socialist promise to support a pro-military social order
and rearmament also proved to be very attractive to the
military. At the same time, the military leadership was
clearly discouraged by the National Socialist insistence
on controlling its own members very tightly and by the
demand of the National Socialist leadership for a leading role in political and military decisions. They
could not, by and large, envision the Nazi movement and
its leaders as equals in government and they were outright opposed to any form of co-determination in military matters, be it from above or from below. Whereas
the military aimed at professional or even sociopolitical autonomy in their pursuit of rearmament,
Hitler very clearly aimed at some kind of political
influence on an element so important to his own options
in the future. At a minimum, he and the Nazi leadership
needed a secure footing in a potential government. By
the same token, they knew very well that they could not
come to power against the military and the presidency -
a telling example for the state of republican affairs
after 1930 - and Hitler made it his main strategy to
gain power legally, that is, with the acquiescence
ultimately of the military leadership.
　　Industry was ambivalent as well. Not only did
"industry" comprise a variety of interests and outlooks,
some of which were quite vividly opposed to one-sided
armaments, but industry as a whole also had to balance,
especially after 1931, a growing interest in state orders (though not necessarily for military procurement of
weapons) with its wide-felt desire to curtail the influence of the state in economic affairs. The wish for
greater autonomy was more a reaction against the republican welfare state - and, for that matter, against
obligations under the Versailles Treaty - but it included a genuine turn against state intervention in favor
of the reduction of the state's role to what was ironically called a "strong state," that is, a state which did
not interfere in production and marketing, but guaranteed the conditions of production, by force if necessary. While industrialists counted socialists and
Communists among the threats to a productive order, and
while they feared the unemployed, they were uncertain

whether or not they should count the Nazis among the un-
savory elements.

The years between 1930 and 1933 were characterized
by a deadlock which was broken by three events: (a) the
beginning of an economic upswing, though slight, in the
second half of 1932, which activated industry; (b) the
potential success of some kind of arms control arrange-
ment, which alarmed and mobilized the military bureaucracy; (c) the potential reforging of ties between the
presidential state and society on the basis of a
Prussian "New Deal" between the Reichswehr Ministry and
social organizations, especially labor, which mobilized
the Nazis and almost everybody else. Despite the highly
uncertain nature of Schleicher's politics, this combination of factors sprang the lock.[10] A compromise between the military with its hold on the presidency under
Hindenburg, Hitler with his power base in a mobilized
society and, secondarily, between the former two and industrial organizations - had to be worked out after the
"Cabinet of National Concentration" was formed. The
search for a compromise shaped the activities in
1933/34.

The emerging compromise distributed gains and los-
ses very unevenly. The Reichswehr became autonomous in
every respect and acted like it. The military almost
instantly took an active stand against any arms control
compromise and blocked even mere face saving contributions to the Disarmament Conference. This policy only
hardened over time. By late 1933 the military leadership was unwilling to accept any arms control compromise
at all. The same hardening of military positions can be
observed in terms of the recruitment of soldiers. Originally plans were circulated that aimed at far reaching
compromises with the National Socialists and, especially, with the paramilitary Sturmabteilung (SA [Storm-
troopers]) on the basis of the revamping of the entire
state structure. All these plans meshed the National
Socialist and the military organization tightly together. (These efforts have their parallel in the various
plans for the corporate reorganization of industry.)
However, the two sides were driven apart on the insti-
gation of conservative officers who demanded complete
military control over all aspects of recruitment through
the introduction of general conscription. The bloody
purge of the SA was one of the results of the agreement
of December 1933 to introduce general conscription at
the earliest possible time.[11]

Neither a polycratic model nor for that matter a
dualistic one of a partnership or, at least, a division
of labor between the military and the political leadership as equals can adequately describe the initial position of the military in the new state. Both nationally
and internationally, the new military leadership pursued
a course of unilateral and speedy rearmament against

which it tolerated little resistance. In fact, while
Field Marshals Werner von Blomberg and Walther von
Reichenau, the leaders of the armed forces, wanted to
compromise and collaborate with the Nazis, the new leadership of the army, Fritsch and Beck, wanted none of
that. They demanded, with the backing of the president,
autonomy and control over the military and all matters
of "national defense." All this can only lead to one
conclusion: if any group came to power in 1933 it was
the Reichswehr, and if any group increased its influence
and control during that year, it was the conservative
leadership of the army under Fritsch and Beck. It
should be noted that both these orthodox military officers attained their positions only in the Third Reich
and that the restoration of the army began in connection
with rearmament.[12] In fact, for the army leadership
rearmament was a prerequisite for restoration which
would be completed with the revision of the
international order.

There was ample room left for the National
Socialist leadership to consolidate its political hold
over Reich, state and communal offices, and over the
streets. These were vast arenas of action for National
Socialists. With them came all kinds of rivalries that
figure so prominently in the polycratic model. Yet the
key issue in the interaction between industry, military,
and the National Socialist leadership remained who controlled armaments.

The Nazi leadership clearly did not control armaments. The suppression of the SA was an indication of
the price which Hitler paid for that fact. (It should
be noted that the ties to the Nazi Mittelstand movement
were relinquished at the same time.) The Nazi movement
and the party were not the same after that. The Nazi
leadership had shifted its power base from the mobilization of society into the state. While the purge
proved to be extremely popular with the population at
large,[13] the ties between National Socialist leadership and social organization in the Nazi party were
weakened and became more indirect than before. They
were increasingly based on ritualized propaganda. The
cleavage between social movement and leadership widened.
The authority and legitimacy of the Nazi leadership now
had to be created on new grounds. The shift into the
state was, moreover, an extremely risky move. It established the top Nazi leadership in a state over which it
had only very partial control, because the most promi-
nent element in that state, the military leadership,
remained autonomous and the issue of the presidency was
not yet settled. Yet Hitler worked his way into military affairs from this nadir in his relations with the
military to a point from which he could risk an open
coup d'état against the orthodox military leadership in
1938. Only by understanding the initial weakness of

Hitler in his relations to the military and the initial triumph of the army leadership (and the most conservative elements in it), can we begin to appreciate the turnaround that followed in the next four years.

How was this turn of events possible? Conventional interpretations point either to conspiracies, to military foolishness, or to the super-human abilities of Hitler as a politician. It seems that the answer lies in the nature of armament. The military was autonomous in its own sphere and, yet, it was dependent on others in the pursuit of rearmament. Most of all, it needed domestic support. The financial means for rearmament had to be provided and the details of financing had to be arranged (involving in this case international action of the Bank for International Settlement as well). Once rearmament was under way, someone had to underwrite the redistributive consequences of massive military spending, which became an issue after 1935/36. The legitimacy of armaments and spending for armaments had to be established. In addition, the scarcity of consumer goods and National Socialist austerity politics[14] became increasingly stringent, as the pace of rearmament quickened. In 1938, it was the military leadership which felt a lack of popular support and yet it knew of no one other than Hitler who could remedy that. Hitler personally, and National Socialist propaganda more generally, became the major legitimating forces for rearmament. They grew into this role with the expansion of rearmament and they gained leverage in this process.

Someone, moreover, had to assure the loyalty of the recruits. Concern about reliability became general when the draft was introduced in 1935. While conscription was absolutely vital in the eyes of the army leadership, it was all the more alarming, since memories of the military strike of 1918 lingered on. Once again, it was the National Socialist regime that guaranteed recruitment and conscription through propaganda and, if necessary, through surveillance and terror. In fact, the trade-offs were more evident in this case than most everywhere else. For the package deal of 1934 is quite evident. While the SA was purged, the Army swore loyalty to Hitler. At the same time, the SS began its ascent in the Nazi state. While the army leadership was very careful in curtailing the growth of a parallel army, it was by no means opposed to an effective militarized police force. On this basis the SS slipped through. By 1938 it was no longer the army which profited from the trade-offs, but Himmler and Hitler. While they still had to compromise (and effectively did so until 1943 -1944), the tables were turned against the military leadership.[15]

Economic support for rearmament was a second factor. Here, matters were complicated by the fact that industry entered as a third autonomous force which had its own rather complex dealings with the Nazi leadership

and the Nazi party. It is noteworthy, though, that
Hitler served, from 1933 on, as high level mediator and
facilitator between army and industry. The selection of
Hjalmar Schacht (Reich Commissioner for National Currency) and the preparations for an armaments package
were part of this mediation. Military economic planners
like Thomas repeatedly asked for Hitler's open and direct leadership in military-economic matters, but this
was always declined. Nevertheless, Hitler's support was
crucial in engineering the two decisive turns in the
evolution of the relations between industry and the
military in 1935/36 and 1938/39. These two turns have
sparked some elaborate debates, yet remarkably little
research.

In brief, Hitler cooperated very closely with the
military leadership in accelerating armaments in 1935/36
against all those elements - among them, heavy industry
- which favored a shift from national to international
recovery (and hence a kind of indexation of armament).
The Four Year Plan under Reichsmarschall Hermann Göring
was an offspring of these negotiations which mostly
centered around direct armaments expenditures in the
context of the army's turn to offensive armaments.[16]
These initiatives had their very complex industrial
support structure as well as their detractors. It is
well known that the chemical industry figured prominently in the preparation and implementation of the Four
Year Plan. It is less well known that the Luftwaffe industries aimed at building up their own support network
with the Plan. Very few would expect to find the capital goods industries behind the Four Year Plan - they
are normally counted among the export industries - even
though its goal of building an independent supply base
for iron and steel, as well as other basic materials,
was one of the few chances to gain their independence
from heavy industrial suppliers who, at the moment, were
exporting iron and steel rather than supplying the armaments industries.[17] These events showed the cooperation of the military and Hitler at high tide. They succeeded in at least partially shaping investment patterns
and, with that, narrowing the future options of industry.[18] Whether they succeeded in accelerating armaments, as Hitler and the armed forces would have liked,
is another matter; for the delays in arms procurement in
1937 indicate that the autonomous control over production and marketing was less seriously jeopardized than
the awesome assembly of laws and regulations would have
us think. In fact, the quota regulation for iron and
steel was used in 1937 against a further expansion of
armaments. (The decision to limit armaments, in turn,
had little to do with resistance but with a blossoming
export market and a favorable price structure.)

Much less has been done to study the second turn in
early 1938, when heavy industry began to push massively
into the domestic armaments market[19] and initiated a

change which eventually led to a complete loss of control over armaments by the military in favor of a civilian munitions ministry. This was a struggle over the
national control of production and marketing (as well as
prices) which was now (1938) dominated by procurement of
weapons. The military soundly lost this conflict. The
Nazi leadership, on the other hand, remained at the very
center of the economic support for rearmament, because
it guaranteed the quietude of workers and the availability of resources. While the National Socialist leadership ran into a host of problems in this respect ever
since 1934/35, there were hardly any substantial alternatives for a different organization of the means of
production. For, despite hassles with the National Socialist leadership and especially with the German Labor
Front, no one in industry pleaded for a return to bargaining with trade unions or for the return to a free
market economy.

Lastly, rearmament had to be guaranteed against a
potentially adverse international environment. Here,
the dependence of the armed forces on Hitler personally
became most glaring. Already in May 1933 Hitler "saved"
the army from the consequences of its unilateral rearma-
ments policies at the Disarmament Conference by turning
to "his" peace initiative which successfully deceived
both the domestic and the international public. With
every step in unilateral rearmament and with every acceleration in that process the dependence of the military on Hitler became more acute. He was the guarantor
of peace as long as the military was not ready to fight
a war. Hitler, in turn, used this accumulated power in
1938 and in 1939 to prod a reluctant army leadership
into war. In fact, it is rather doubtful that foreign
policy fell automatically to Hitler, as if he only had
to usurp and keep it. It was unilateral rearmament and
the military search for someone to support and guarantee
that policy that pulled him into that position. Hitler
maintained and increased his hold over foreign policy in
step with the intensification and acceleration of rearmament. By 1938/39 one can indeed speak of his near
absolute control over that domain.

The military, in sum, started out as an autonomous
body in the Third Reich. There is even good reason to
believe that it actually was the dominant power, though
that may be disputed. In any event, it lost much of its
power within the next four to five years. These years
were not characterized by any frontal assault of the
Nazi leadership or the rank and file against the military, even though the army leadership pursued a pronoun-
cedly restorative course. Rather, these years were
marked by the tremendous expansion of the armed forces
on the basis of what was a remarkably encompassing division of labor with the Nazi leadership, which started
out as the distinctly weaker partner in this alliance.

However, the alliance around rearmament was also the
major source of the Wehrmacht's problems. For the military needed the Nazi leadership in order to guarantee
rearmament. This was all the more the case since the
restorative army leadership insisted on the strict seg-
regation of state and society, the hierarchical organization of control, and the domination of the military
over society. Hence, we can conclude that the faster
and the more intense rearmament became, and the further
the reconstruction of the military institution progressed, the deeper became the dependence. The influence of Hitler on military affairs grew with massive
unilateral rearmament.

What are the consequences of these observations?
Most importantly, the mere portrayal of the relations
between traditional elites and the Nazi movement falls
short of what actually happened whether we explain these
relations according to a polycratic model or in terms of
a traditional dualism between the military and the political leadership. Least successful is a Hitler-centered
interpretation - not necessarily because Hitler did not
have decisive influence, but because this interpretation
never questions how and when he got it. These interpretations fall short - at least as far as the relations
between traditional elites and the National Socialist
leadership are concerned - because they portray a remarkably passive and bureaucratic picture of the power
struggles in the Third Reich. Power is allotted or as-
cribed, but it is never acquired or maintained. It is a
very abstract and ethereal construct - more akin to
status than to actual control over resources and the
ability to impose one's own interests on others. This,
however, was the major battlefront in the Third Reich.
The single most important factor that impinged on an
otherwise quite immaculate autonomy of the military was
the necessity to organize violence on a quickly expand-
ing scale if the armed forces wanted to fight a war.
This military interest in war may very well be interpreted in terms of an inherited Grossmachtstreben
(though it does not need to be interpreted in terms of
traditions), but the will to power does not explain what
moved the Third Reich or for that matter Europe.

Rearmament did. It entailed the organization of
society and material resources and their transformation
into means of destruction. This was a process of con-
tinuously exerting power over society and economy. The
control over the means of destruction involved the military in a whole series of power relations and power
struggles with industry, social, and political organizations. It was by no means clear who would dominate
these relations, and we must wonder why the military
lost out, while industry and Nazi leadership prevailed.
For even after it had lost the backing of the presidency, the military still had a number of advantages. Not

only did it have prestige and status which was celebrat-
ed and heightened by propaganda, but it provided orders
for weapons as well (as long as it was able to control
procurement); it could create an aura of strength and
thus reinforce the image of the nation; and, last but
not least, it could give the promise of war. On the
other hand, the military - and the militarily orthodox
officers more than anyone else - had serious liabilities. Ultimately, it lacked control over the production
of weapons, because it did not control the means of
production. It had, moreover, lost faith in its ability
to control society as well. These factors were com-
pounded by a third. Despite the high percentage of
aristocratic officers, the officer corps never had a
solid base in the upper classes of German society after
1918, and it is very dubious whether the majority of
officers wanted these tight links to a particular class.
The German officer corps conceived of itself as a
professional rather than an aristocratic corps. Aristocratic and non-aristocratic officers alike gained their
status not from where they came from, but from what they
did. Hence, one might very well argue that the problems
of the military in the Third Reich derived very much
from the fact that it was not a traditional force.

This army and this officer corps depended entirely
on armament and on the legitimacy of the organization of
violence. The emphasis on military action rather than
on social status may explain, on the one hand, why they
were so radically opposed to anyone who even remotely
doubted the value of the military organization and why
they leaned so heavily on those who provided support.
This kind of radicalization of the military - due to the
loss of a solid social backing in a dominant class and
due to its conversion into a "service" - is a general
feature of most European armies (though it is a controversial issue among German historians). What is different and new in the Third Reich is the unregulated
process of bartering advantages and making trade-offs in
the process of using power in organizing violence; the
devolution of political power to autonomous power holders; and the dissolution of boundaries between state,
society, and economy. The resulting exchange relations
counted in the Third Reich rather more than the mere
ascription of power to bureaucratic positions or traditional elites. The active competition and the bargaining over power relations was a relatively recent phenomenon in German politics that distinguished it from the
nineteenth century affairs of a bureaucratized state and
aristocratized military institution. This difference
was further enhanced after 1933 by the destruction of
any ordered political processes. This destruction,
though, was quite as much a result of the military
search for autonomy as it was a consequence of the
National Socialist rise to power.

III.

We instantly have to add a caveat to these observations. We tried to demonstrate a principle by looking at one of the so-called traditional elites, the military, more carefully. In developing a full picture of the rise of Nazism and its relations to the established powers in industry and the state we would have to blend the military organization of violence and its contingencies with the National Socialist problems of providing legitimacy for the new regime and acquiring authority, which was mostly lacking in 1933 - at least in the eyes of the military and of industry. We would instantly discover how much the National Socialist leadership was dependent on industry and, ultimately, on the military - not in the simplistic sense of being their pawn, but in the sense that industry had to produce again and employ workers and the military had to be able to actually fight a war after the completion of rearmament. We would also have to look at industry, its tenuous control over the factors of production, and its search for profitability. We would discover the debt which industry owed to the National Socialist leadership in securing control and in improving profitability, and we would see in this context the initially slow, and after 1938, explosive growth in importance of armaments contracts in maintaining profitability. It may suffice here to have outlined some principles for studying the relations between traditional elites and National Socialist leaders by looking at one protagonist in some more detail. A study of the exchanges on the emerging National Socialist "power market" is still lacking. It seems one of the most important tasks of a new political history of the Third Reich.

Unfortunately, even an extended study along these lines would not cover the whole story. In the cases of two of the protagonists, the military and industry, the portrayal of the ensuing conflicts over power and control would suffice. For as long as the organization of violence and the organization of production were guaranteed, everything else was of only marginal importance to them (even though the guarantee of production and destruction had rather far-reaching implications). Conditions were quite different for the Nazi leadership and Hitler. Not only did their power and influence depend on the authority and legitimacy of the regime, but there is good reason to believe that they considered the reconstruction of society as a prerequisite for its stability and, hence, for the survival of their regime. While there is considerable debate on the nature of that prospective society,[20] and debate on the link between reconstruction, war, and annihilation is just beginning,[21] there is little doubt that war was the decisive means to that end.[22] However these issues may be

resolved, the quest for a new society put the National
Socialist leadership more at odds with both industry and
the military than anything else. In fact, it was the
perceived need for revamping German society that gave
the entire power struggle between the military, industry, and the political leadership in the Third Reich a
completely new dimension and a polarity which surfaced
only slowly.

The two consequences which result from the opposing
rationales for political conflict are worth noting. The
first one concerns the use of terror. Neither industry
nor the military hesitated in the least to use coercion,
repression, and even outright terror in organizing violence and production against any effective or potential
resistance. The institutionalization of terror, moreover, was not new. In fact, it was very much an inven-
tion of the militarily backed counterrevolution in
1918/19. Wehrmacht as well as industry cooperated
gladly with the Gestapo and the emerging SS state in
1933/34. Yet there remained a difference between the
military and industry on one side, the Nazi security
apparatus on the other. Industry and the military were
interested in "functional" terror and repression. They
wanted their operations run smoothly and, when this
required force, they were ready to employ it. For the
National Socialist leadership terror became a means of
creating a new society through indirect coercion and
through direct and physical exploitation, even annihilation.[23] The shared interest in coercion and terror
and the division over the roles of the military and the
Nazi security agencies were evident from very early on
in the regime. But the conflict became a matter of open
concern only after the 1938/39 period, when terror
became more manifest with Kristallnacht and then the
emergence of the Einsatzgruppen (SS killing squads) in
Poland. The new terrorism revealed the shift in power
relations that had occurred since 1933, when the
National Socialist leadership could proceed to realize
their plans for the future without significant
resistance.

The second consequence concerns the relation between state and society. The purge of the SA in 1934
meant that the direct relationship between National
Socialist leadership and mobilized society was tempo-
rarily weakened while the positions of the army and
industrial leadership were confirmed. The Nazi leadership used the interval to build a power base in the
state apparatus. Subsequently Hitler was to take advantage of rearmament and then the war to strive to reforge
the bond between the Nazi leadership and society. This
aspiration lay behind the coup d'etat against the military leadership in 1938, and behind Hitler's insistence
on war at the earliest possible date. General Ludwig
Beck, the Chief of the General Staff, openly challenged

the Nazi leadership by demanding that instrumental
rationality should prevail in the decision concerning
war and peace (that is, war could only be fought when
the military deemed itself to be ready), while Hitler
insisted on the primacy of his ideological goals for
reshaping the social order. When Hitler won in this
conflict, it was obvious that the tide had turned. The
National Socialist leadership had seized the initiative
which effectively meant war at the earliest possible
date and it meant ideological war, a Weltanschauungskrieg[24] at that. A Weltanschauungskrieg was not
simply a war with ideological undertones - that is, the
traditional outlook of the military plus the fanaticism
of the National Socialist leadership. Rather, it was a
war that aimed at the destruction of other societies
(rather than at the "functional" defeat of the strategic
concentrations of enemy forces) in order to facilitate
the rebuilding of one's own. Ultimately, this was a
quest for an autonomous society that lived off and
regenerated itself through the exploitation of others.
To that end it needed production and destruction and
their specialists - and the National Socialist regime
found them because, in the eyes of the traditional
elites, it seemed to be better able to uphold the necessary conditions for production and destruction than any
other regime. This advantage far outweighed any liabilities that came with the growing polarity of strategies in organizing society for the majority of the
traditional elites.

NOTES

1. See the debate on the issue in Gerhard
Hirschfeld and Lothar Kettenacker, eds., Der
"Führerstaat": Mythos und Realität. Studien zur Struktur
und Politik des Dritten Reiches (Stuttgart: Klett-Cotta,
1981).

2. Horst Boog et al., eds., Der Angriff auf die
Sowjetunion (Stuttgart: Deutsche Verlagsanstalt, 1983
[Das Deutsche Reich und der Zweite Weltkrieg, Vol. 4]).

3. Klaus-Jürgen Müller, Das Heer und Hitler.
Armee und nationalsozialistisches Regime 1933-1940
(Stuttgart: Deutsche Verlagsanstalt, 1969) or, more
recently, A. Hillgruber, "Die Reichswehr und das
Scheitern der Weimarer Republik," in Karl D. Erdmann and
Hagen Schulze, eds., Weimar, Selbstpreisgabe einer
Demokratie (Düsseldorf: Droste, 1980), 177-92.

4. Wilhelm Deist et al., eds., Ursachen und Voraussetzungen der deutschen Kriegspolitik (Stuttgart: Deutsche Verlagsanstalt, 1979 [Das Deutsche Reich und der Zweite Weltkrieg, Vol. 1]).

5. Manfred Messerschmidt, Die Wehrmacht im NS Staat. Zeit der Indoktrination (Hamburg: R.V. Decker Verlag, 1969).

6. Fritz Fischer, Bündnis der Eliten. Zur Kontinuität der Machtstrukturen in Deutschland 1871-1945 (Düsseldorf: Droste, 1979), especially 92ff.

7. Klaus Hildebrand, Das Dritte Reich (Munich: Oldenbourg, 1980), with a summary in favor of the Hitlerist approach.

8. Ulrich Heinemann, Die verdrängte Niederlage. Politische Öffentlichkeit und Kriegsschuldfrage in der Weimarer Republik (Göttingen: Vandenhoeck and Ruprecht, 1983).

9. Ian Kershaw, Der Hitler Mythos. Volksmeinung und Propaganda im Dritten Reich (Stuttgart: Deutsche Verlagsanstalt, 1980) as well as his Popular Opinion and Political Dissent in the Third Reich Bavaria 1933-1945 (Oxford: Clarendon 1983).

10. Axel Schildt, Militärdiktatur mit Massenbasis? Die Querfrontkonzeption der Reichswehrführung um General von Schleicher am Ende der Weimarer Republik (Frankfurt/Main and New York: Campus, 1981).

11. An excellent summary for the years 1931-1933 is Edward W. Bennett, German Rearmament and the West, 1932-1933 (Princeton: Princeton University Press, 1979).

12. In some detail: Karl-Jürgen Müller, General Ludwig Beck. Studien und Dokumente zur politisch-militärischen Vorstellungswelt und Tätigkeit des Generalstabschefs des deutschen Heeres 1933-1938 (Boppard: Boldt, 1980).

13. Kershaw, Hitler-Mythos, 72-80.

14. Fritz Blaich, "Wirtschaft und Rüstung in Deutschland 1933-1939," in Wolfgang Benz and Hermann Graml, eds., Sommer 1939. Die Grossmächte und der europäische Krieg (Stuttgart: Deutsche Verlagsanstalt, 1979), 35-59.

15. Wolfgang Kern, Die innere Funktion der Wehrmacht (Berlin, GDR: Militärverlag, 1979) and Bernd Wegner, Hitlers politische Soldaten; Die Waffen SS 1933-1945 (Paderborn: Schöningh, 1982).

16. Wilhelm Deist, The Wehrmacht and German Rearmament (London and Basingstoke: Macmillan, 1981).

17. Michael Geyer, "Der Einfluss der national-sozialistischen Rüstungspolitik auf das Ruhrgebiet," Rheinische Vierteljahrsblätter 45 (1981): 201-64.

18. Dietmar Petzina, Autarkiepolitik im Dritten Reich; Der nationalsozialistische Vierjahresplan, 1936-1941 (Stuttgart: Deutsche Verlagsanstalt, 1968).

19. Michael Geyer, "Rüstungsbeschleunigung und Inflation. Zur Inflationsdenkschrift des OKW vom November 1938," Militärgeschichtliche Mitteilungen 2 (1981): 121-86.

20. Jeffrey Herf, "Reactionary Modernism: Some Ideological Origins of the Primacy of Politics in the Third Reich," Theory and Society 10 (November 1981): 805-32 and E. Hennig, Bürgerliche Gesellschaft und Faschismus in Deutschland (Frankfurt/Main: Suhrkamp, 1977).

21. Eric Goldhagen, "Weltanschauung und Endlösung," Vierteljahrshefte für Zeitgeschichte vol. 24, no. 4 (1976): 379-405.

22. Ludolf Herbst, Der totale Krieg und die Ordnung der Wirtschaft. Die Kriegswirtschaft im Spannungsfeld von Politik, Ideologie und Propaganda 1939-1945 (Stuttgart: Deutsche Verlagsanstalt, 1982).

23. See, for example, Hitler's remarks in front of officers and generals on May 26, 1944; partly edited in Hans H. Wilhelm, "Wie geheim war die Endlösung?" in Wilhelm Benz et al., eds., Miscellanea: Festschrift für H. Krausnick (Stuttgart: Deutsche Verlagsanstalt, 1980), 131-48, especially 134-36.

24. Boog, Der Angriff, see especially 413-50.

10
Discussion

Following the presentations of Jane Caplan, Michael
Geyer and Hans Mommsen, Charles Maier, who chaired the
discussion, offered several comments on the Nazi economy. But in order to address such questions as, "Is the
Nazi economy revolutionary?", "Who benefits who los-
es?", and "Is it capitalism?", Maier suggested that the
definition of capitalism be spelled out. If by capitalism one means the right to enjoy certain revenues derived from private property, Maier said, then, with the
exception of "Aryanization," Nazism did not disrupt
capitalism. If capitalism means the right to define
decision-making within the sphere of production that a
particular industrialist controls, Nazism could be said
to have actually reinforced capital, Maier stated. But
if by capitalism one means that those who control certain assets of production have a commanding voice in the
formulation of national policy, then one would say that
Nazism "seriously eroded" capitalism in Germany. That
was the trade-off Nazism gave capitalists, Maier concluded: enhanced private control and diminished public
control.

On the issue of rearmament, Maier concurred with
Michael Geyer that the economic turnaround preceded
rearmament. Maier noted the debate between the
thesis represented by Burton Klein, then Alan Milward,
that performance was not too great, and that the early
rearmament effort was overestimated, and Richard Overy's
assessment that Germany spent considerably more than
other European nations and was getting ready for an even
greater effort.

Maier stated that Nazism was successful at recover-
ing from the depression, but not terribly successful at
managing a national economy. Maier attributed this to
the structure and ideology of the Nazi regime. Both
ideology and structure worked well to move a country
from a point of under-capacity, but were not able to
"prioritize" when mobilizing for war and fighting the
war itself. The fascist ideology was one of maximiza-
tion, Maier said. It could stimulate growth. The Nazis

had "absolutely no capacity and real procedure for pri-
oritization when they were at the threshold of producing
to capacity."

William Allen differed with Maier on the explanation for the performance of the Nazi regime, noting that
the machinery of power in the Nazi party was suited to
vote-getting, not government.

Christopher Jackson observed that Hitler attempted
to solve problems in ways that did not have costs.
Jackson illustrated his point with the example of the
food shortage in 1936: Hitler's solution was to "can
food, which was no solution, "rather than make a reduction in arms or other spending. Jackson said that
everything was to be done in the future, and that the
territory captured during the war was to provide vast
resources.

Anson Rabinbach attributed the Nazis' lack of
ability to prioritize to the fact the Nazis' "ideological concerns were constantly conflicting with, and
contra-factual to, the political aims" of the regime
itself. In supporting this point, Rabinbach noted three
different war aims of the Nazis: defeating the enemy,
colonizing the East, and solving the "Jewish question."
Rabinbach thought it important to document at what times
one or another of these goals had priority.

David Kaiser added that, in the early years of the
regime, much was obscured by the need to move slowly.
Only later on did decisions come to reflect Hitler's
priorities. From his own work on foreign trade policy,
Kaiser commented that all policy came to reflect Nazi
ideology.

MacGregor Knox said that Germany's performance was
good compared to the "mediocre" effort of the Italians,
and attributed this difference to the German military
tradition.

Henry Turner interjected that the heavy industries' lack of interest in rearmament was due to an
overriding interest in reducing state spending and taxa-
tion. Turner also emphasized the Nazis' use of terror
in any explanation of industry behavior, highlighting
state control of business in the Nazi regime.

Jeff Weintraub explored the relation between state
and army under Nazism. Weintraub noted that Hitler gave
the army the resources it wanted, but destroyed its
influence over national policy. On the integrity of the
army itself, Weintraub said that Hitler made general
strategic decisions, but that the Nazis did not interfere with the army's "internal structure." Nazi ideology, furthermore, played almost no role within the army.
Weintraub noted Morris Janowitz and Edward Shil's thesis
about the traditional ethos of the officer corps, and
the small unit cohesion which accounted for its
strength. Weintraub added that, as the war progressed,
Hitler did exercise more control within the army, exem-

plified by the cashiering of several officers, but that this nevertheless contrasted sharply with the Russian army, which lost all semblance of internal control.

David Kaiser differed with Weintraub, stating that the Nazis broke all their promises to the army.

Joseph Rovan said that class analysis is strained in an application to the Nazi regime. Rovan commented that the NSDAP ought to be seen as an organization of "outlaws," and that the Nazi state belongs in the category of "oriental despotism."

In a comment directed to Mommsen and Caplan, Michael Kater noted that functionalism and intentionalism are "misnomers," being too extreme, and asked whether there might be a middle ground between them. Kater suggested that one examine the kinds of decisions Hitler made at certain times, and the sorts of things with which he occupied himself. Kater offered the example of Hitler's decisions to allow or not to allow someone to meet with him. As a guide to Hitler's thinking, he also cited a July 1943 letter from Wilhelm Frick (Minister of the Interior), in which he urged officials not to centralize decision making, a directive Frick took to be in accordance with "the principle of the Führer."

Caplan concurred with Kater that functionalism and intentionalism are not satisfactory, but did not agree with Kater on the meaning of Frick's communication. Caplan said that Frick was in fact the "arch-centralizer," and that he announced his aversion to centralization to mask his intention to take the opposite course.

Caplan concluded with her view of Hitler and his relation to the bureaucracy. "Hitler," Caplan argued, "created a space he could not in practice fill." Caplan illustrated this point with a "hopelessly naive statement by Hans Frank (Hitler's legal adviser, later head of the general government in occupied Poland) who got very interested in administrative problems in the early 1940s." Frank explained the need for bureaucracy in the following way, Caplan said: "If Hitler could do everything, of course, he would. But since he could not practically do everything, you had to have a bureaucracy, you had to have some kind of administration." That, Caplan said, was the ethos of bureaucratic organization in the Nazi regime. The bureaucracy, Caplan concluded, was

> simply...so many little Hitlers, as it were, atomized, parceled out to do the Führer's will. That produces an identity, a space, a location for Hitler which he can not pursue in practice, you can not find him in this illusory position of doing everything. I think you can find plenty of evidence that the regime itself had some, perhaps not enough, sense of its own irrationality and contradictions, and that it was working with this kind of role.

Geyer cautioned that neither the military nor industry should be seen as consolidated blocs. Geyer said that both were internally threatened, and that this opened them to Nazi ideology. "The majority of officers was willing to forsake a great deal of autonomy, and was certainly also willing to forsake its veto power over strategic decisions," Geyer said. Geyer viewed the relation between the army and the NSDAP as one in which the army links with a group of people "with which it has no affinity and no interest, but it [the NSDAP] provides a number of things, and that is the tension which I think is essential."

Maier commented that the "outlaw band" was not adequate for the analysis of government in Germany:

> Robin Hood lives in the woods. He does not have to run a state. He can take from the state and do what he wants....When the outlaw band meets the whole matrix of a very complicated social, economic, and political system, then you have some interactions that you have to think about in other terms.

Maier concluded that the distinction between core areas of Hitler's concern and those he left to clientelism is a useful one. Lastly, Maier registered a reluctance to select between functionalism and intentionalism: "Why should one word serve us?" Maier asked, "I think of this as a sort of fragmented type of decisionism."

11
Women Between God and Führer

Claudia Koonz

"Resistance" calls to mind the heroic plots and
organized clandestine activities in the face of massive
repression during the Second World War. Within the context of 1933-1936, however, what does the term really
mean? We know many Germans said "No." Over half of the
German electorate refused to vote for the Nazi regime in
March 1933 despite massive terror and propaganda; about
800,000 Germans spent time in jails or concentration
camps during 1933; Communists and Socialists established
networks for protest and rescue work; and nearly 60,000
Jews left Germany in the first months of Nazi power. At
the other end of the political spectrum, nearly 14 million voters supported National Socialist candidates in
the July 1932 elections and a million and a half Germans
belonged to the National Socialist Party when Hindenburg
appointed Hitler Chancellor. A year later that total
had more than doubled. These Germans said some form of
"Yes" to the new rulers.
     But what of the millions who were neither in the
party nor in jail or exile? These Germans "in the middle" mean little to historians of political elites because they did not launch major protests or seriously
threaten Nazi power. Moreover, any history of the inar-
ticulate and essentially passive majority in a police
state confronts staggering methodological difficulties.[1] However, as social historians, our central
questions focus on just this "gray" area as we analyze
responses to Nazi policies and patterns of compliance
and sources of protest among Germans who considered
themselves neither fanatics nor opponents of the Nazi
regime.[2] The history of women in the Third Reich sup-
plies us with crucial information and insights in this
area of inquiry.[3] These questions cannot be answered
without an understanding of women's responses to the
Third Reich. Of course, as half of the population,
women are important as historical subjects. But, in
addition, women interpreted Nazi society from a unique
perspective and left records that provide us with a rich

array of primary sources. In this essay, I will summarize the responses of traditional, non-socialist women
to Hitler's takeover. Because these women generally
welcomed Hitler's chancellorship, they certainly do not
belong in the category, "resistance;" yet because they
soon withdrew their support, they cannot be considered
as supporters, either.

Middle-class women, from whom Nazis drew their
support, tended to join organizations that remained (at
least officially) above party controversy. Gleich-
schaltung, therefore, had little impact on their organizations which (unlike men's politically oriented associations) remained legal after 1933. Fortunately for
historians, their archives were not destroyed and their
officials continued to collect documentation. Despite
heavy censorship, the memos and reports in these archives are astonishingly frank. Women in Nazified organizations knew that they needed reliable feedback in
order to do their duty well, and they routinely ex-
changed self-criticisms and evaluations of their programs. Several factors, however, inhibited their communication - but enriched our source material. Because
women in both church and state bureaucracies suffered
from chronic under-funding, they could not travel or use
long-distance telephone to exchange their private opin-
ions as readily as their male counterparts. In addition, some leaders' husbands did not allow them to move
near their workplace and leave their homes, an incon-
venience which necessitated written memos instead of
conversation. The lowly clerk typist compensated for
all these problems - and generated extensive files
which, for the most part, have not been collected by
national or regional archives.

These sources provide an important perspective on
Nazi society. Although they did not make major policy
decisions, women occupied positions at the interface
between public and private - between family and state,
personal and political. In the late 1920s when traditionally oriented women described this special place,
they often adapted the term Lebensraum which connoted to
them women's special mission to create social harmony
among all classes, regions and religions.[4] Especially
in the turmoil of the Depression, women saw it as their
duty to create a social "space" of interclass harmony
where all members of a community sacrificed for the common good. Men, they said, marched against the Bolshevik
menace; but women alone could fashion a peaceful
domestic "living room."

In the Nazi State, women carried out the mandate to
organize Glaube (faith) and Betreuung (nurturing) and to
create an alltäglicher Lebensraum (everyday domain)
which would mask terror, brutality, and coercion. In
practical terms, the government depended upon women to
indoctrinate the youth, boycott Jewish stores, select

candidates for sterilization, inculcate eugenic ideas, and dispense charity to the worthy poor. As members of the second largest Nazi bureaucracy, they reinforced a sense of Gemeinschaft among the racially "chosen" and ostracized those who did not "belong." The Nazi state rested as surely on the separation of the sexes as upon the exclusion of the Jews. A totalitarian society could not operate without its female half; and the history of that society will not be complete until women's participation in that society had been studied.

In my research, I have examined three national networks of women who generally welcomed Nazi power in 1933: organized Nazi, Catholic, and Protestant women. When historians investigate the origins of Nazism, they frequently compare the Nazi Party with other parties; but in focusing on women, I chose to draw my comparisons between religious organizations and the Nazi movement because in many ways religious networks offered to women the same kinds of communal ties that men enjoyed in political associations. True to stereotypes, women put their faith in the Führer while men fought for him.

Although women in religious and Nazi organizations expressed relief when Hitler became Chancellor, religious women's expectations differed slightly from Nazi women's aspirations. Catholic and Protestant women looked to an authoritarian state to strengthen the "man's world," by ending cultural decadence, providing economic stability, and restoring nationalist fervor. They expected Hitler would "shore up" the social setting in which women functioned so they might more effectively pursue their feminine aims outside the government sphere. Nazi women differed in their expectation that Hitler's state would grant them new powers to intervene in all areas of the women's Lebensraum and saturate it with Nazi ideals and programs. Religious women hoped the position of the individual husband and father would be strengthened; Nazi women expected the state would assume responsibilities over family life as individual men defaulted. Religious women, in short, still saw the patriarchal family as a bulwark against political intrusion; Nazi women regarded the family as their entry to private life.

NATIONAL SOCIALISTS

Until the July elections of 1932, women in the party had enjoyed an autonomy unparalleled in religious women's organizations. So completely did Nazi men ignore them, that they were not even urged to join the party, pay dues, or form a single nationwide association. From this it followed that women Nazis enjoyed considerable autonomy to fashion their own separate political ideologies and organizational techniques. To be sure, they despised the Treaty of Versailles, embraced racism, adored the Führer and hated Bolshevism. And they repeatedly disavowed any claim to "masculine" political or economic "turf." But beneath guise of subservience, they worked for women's concerns within the broader framework of the Nazi Sammelpartei (catchall politics). While swearing utter obedience to the "masculine will," they communicated a secondary message which glorified woman's power within her own Lebensraum (including Kinder, Küche, Kirche plus two more "K's", Krankenhaus und Kultur: children, kitchen, church, hospital and culture). Paradoxically, men's very misogyny provided women Nazis with the illusion that they exercised power over their own realm. A cursory overview of some national leaders' doctrines and styles will illustrate the diversity which, by default, was tolerated in the Nazi movement before 1933.

One early leader, Elsbeth Zander, operated in a charismatic and dictatorial style - swearing total allegiance to the Führer, while insisting on absolute obedience from the "brown sisters" in her Order of the Red Swastika. Zander did her best to win support from the Nazi elite, and succeeded despite her scandalous personal life and her proposal in 1932 to include women candidates on Nazi slates. Guida Diehl, by contrast, admired Hitler but remained staunchly independent of the party organization until 1931. During World War I, she had launched an anti-vice crusade, the "Newland movement." Directing her efforts at well-educated, middle-class mothers, she demanded the elimination of women from wage labor outside the home, endorsed women's disenfranchisement in general national elections, favored a representative parliamentary body elected by women only, and recommended state subsidies for mothers whose husbands could not support them. Besides these two "motherly" figures (both of whom were in their late fifties) two much younger women appealed to followers in their teens and twenties. Racist journalist Sophie Rogge-Boerner praised "Aryan" women as the equals of "their" men, and scorned women of the "lower" races for their inferiority to "their" men. Lydia Gottschewski, the forceful organizer of girls and young women for Hitler, proclaimed her intent to found a tightly integrated women's community to balance male bonding in the SA. Wide discrepancies among regional and local leaders existed as well. But "mothers" and "daughters," atheists and Christians, proponents and opponents of women's economic independence, organized and thought as they wished, without fear of leaders' censure.

All welcomed the prospect of a dictatorship, and planned to utilize the state to expand women's power over their separate sphere. Starting with the Strasser reforms in 1931-32, male leaders began to display some interest in women Nazis. At first women welcomed the improvement of their status; quickly they came to regret their loss of independence; and after January 1933, they lost any hope of autonomy. Five women served as national leaders of the Nazi women's bureaucracy during 1933; Hitler and his deputies had planned for appointments to all major government offices, but they had given no thought at all to women. By the end of that year, all early leaders from the Kampfzeit had been dismissed, and one Herr Krummacher occupied the leading position.

Any leader of the women's bureaucracy presented Nazi leaders with two intrinsic dilemmas. A competent and energetic chief of the Frauenwerk would attract millions of workers and volunteers to her programs; but her very success might well exacerbate male paranoia about the "women's world" which lay outside their "natural" bailiwick. If she were married, she would owe her first loyalty to her husband; but a single woman would not present the correct image. A male leader (married or not) would make women feel slighted. In Frau Gertrud Scholtz-Klink, Nazi leaders resolved the dilemma. Besides presenting the ideal "racial" image so rare among Hitler and his associates, she was a mother without a husband. In fact, she had joined the Nazi movement to replace her fanatical Nazi husband who had died of a heart attack during the excitement of a rally. In her mid-thirties, she came to the task of organizing German women without much previous experience and proved to be an utterly docile figurehead from 1934 to 1945. After Scholtz-Klink took office, old-time women Nazis expressed disillusionment at their leaders' lack of concern for women's issues; at the petty and mercenary attitude of party officials; and at women's loss of autonomy. The fanatic alte Kämpferinnen were replaced by more "respectable" and pragmatic women from more solidly middle-class backgrounds. As bureaucracy supplanted charisma, and male control usurped women's autonomy, the dedicated women leaders who had crusaded against democracy now found themselves excluded from dictatorship.

WOMEN IN PROTESTANT ORGANIZATIONS

While old-time Nazi women confronted the bitter realities of Hitler's "new state" during 1933, Protestant women rejoiced at the Nazi takeover. In part, their enthusiasm stemmed from the expectation that Hitler would deal harshly with atheism and Communism. Partly, too, Protestant women responded to recent Nazi campaign propaganda which stressed the harmony between Nazism and Christianity. Political neutrality, Protestant Women's Association President Paula Mueller-Otfried declared, had been appropriate under Weimar because Protestants deplored the democracy. Now, however, that they lived under a political regime they respected, they

looked forward to close cooperation with the state.
With few regrets, Protestant women's organizations re-
quested their "racially" Jewish members to resign and
supported eugenics programs which the progressive social
workers in church welfare programs had long endorsed.
In addition to genuine enthusiasm, another factor operated. Women leaders calculated that their early devo-
tion to the "new state" would yield rewards for their
organizations - in the form of state grants, autonomy,
and responsibilities within the Nazi health, welfare and
educational systems. After a year of Nazi rule, however, their euphoria dissolved. Many longtime women
leaders insisted they could support Nazi policies without actually joining the party; others balked at the
ideas that a majority of their officers had to join the
NS <u>Frauenschaft</u> and that agendas required party
approval. These stalwarts resigned. But even the more
compliant women who replaced them were aghast when
Hitler deputized a fanatic German Christian, Hans
Hermenau, to lead the Protestant Frauenwork. When it
came to a showdown, Agnes von Grone, leader of over two
million Protestant women, rejected both the German
Christians and the National Bishop. She also insisted
on her impeccable Nazi credentials and disavowed any
connection with the Confessing Church. One could be a
loyal Nazi, she believed, without becoming utterly sub-
servient. She was wrong. Although over three-quarters
of all districts supported her, in late 1935 the Party
Court expelled her from both the party and her position.

WOMEN IN CATHOLIC ORGANIZATIONS

Although they generally called for an authoritarian
solution to Germany's problems, Catholic women prior to
1933 had vigorously opposed Hitler's racial views, contempt for religion, and misogyny. However, they con-
soled themselves after July 1933, thinking that Catholic
prelates would use the Concordat to protect them from
Nazi interference. Assuming their autonomy would continue, they participated in government projects such as
the women's labor corps, motherhood education, and aid
to mothers. Two of their leaders, Antonie Hopmann and
Elisabeth Denis, urged Catholic women to keep their
organizational integrity but work with the state. When,
however, the chief of Catholic Charities told them to
cooperate with eugenics programs and to allow Nazis to
appoint their leaders, indoctrinate the youth, examine
their financial records, and attend their meetings; they
withdrew their good will. In early 1933, they had stood
willing to serve Nazi goals, but only as long as these
goals did not impinge on specifically Catholic doctrine
or organizations. Using "purely religious" format, many

Catholic women utilized retreats, bible societies, altar
care committees, and reading circles to maintain their
faith beyond Gestapo surveillance. Many also simply
yielded to the order of the day.

Catholic and Protestant women who in March 1933 had
declared their willingness to serve the new state -
women who hated democracy and craved authority, patri-
archy, and community - these women within three years
had withdrawn from the Nazi consensus. Starting in
1934-35, women church leaders faced double disillusionment as it became clear that the state aimed at under-
cutting the last shreds of their organizational integrity and that the male church from which they expected
protection urged its women's organizations to cooperate.
Thus, when national women's leaders objected (and they
virtually always did) they faced both government and
state with varying degrees of obstinacy. Very
generally, I would suggest that motherhood oriented
associations proved the most susceptible to Nazi orders
while certain occupational groups (notably teachers) remained the most resistant to policies and leaders of
whom they did not approve.[5] Women who accepted anti-
Semitism, nationalist indoctrination, political terror,
and repression, drew the line when the state jeopardized
their own organizational power. Like the old-time women
Nazi leaders, these women did not often conspire against
the Nazi regime after becoming disillusioned; but they
expressed their dissent, waged bureaucratic struggles,
inhibited the efficient functioning of some programs,
and withdrew their endorsement from Hitler's government.
Except for Catholic women who opposed eugenic policies,
these women embraced Hitler's social goals and ideology
but objected to the Nazi state.

CONCLUSIONS

Nazi women before 1933, like organized church women
during the early years of Nazi power, enjoyed a brief
period of harmony within Nazi organizations as long as
they assumed they would receive authority to expand
their "feminine" Lebensraum. They did not want "an
escape from freedom" as much as an escape from male
oversight. Experience, not willful myopia, explains
this misperception, for until Nazi leaders took cogni-
zance of women, women did operate independently.
Women's relationships with the Nazi Party between 1928
and 1935 contribute to findings made by recent scholarship which emphasize the role of grassroots organizing
(rather than Hitler's charisma) as the secret of Nazi
success. The records of generally pro-Nazi women suggest that despite Hitler's boasting about his "iron
will" and the "leadership principle," the explanation

for the Nazis' spectacular electoral successes among men
and women lay elsewhere. Gregor Strasser, the master-
mind of party organization, suggested in 1932 that it
was precisely the absence of fixed dogma or clear chains
of command which provided ambitious, young, local
leaders with sufficient scope for their energies.[6]
Throughout Germany, Strasser continued, "an entirely new
type of preacher-soldier" had emerged to carry the Nazi
faith into the tiniest hamlet and the poorest slum.
Although Strasser did not refer to women in this memo,
his observations help to explain women's enthusiasm for
National Socialism. Nazi leaders' apathy gave ambitious
and often rebellious women the chance to pioneer in the
creation of new organizations independent of established
women's associations and male oversight. Had he thought
about women, Strasser might well have noticed another
"unique" type: the preacher-mother, who adapted her
rhetoric and organizational strategies to local conditions and elaborated her own political style; who often
indulged in "male" behavior like smuggling weapons or
marching past hecklers, in the name of traditional women's roles; and who dreamed of organizing motherhood
for national glory.

If Strasser was correct, it would follow that the
less important the organization, the greater its autonomy. This placed women at the bottom of the status
hierarchy but at the top on the autonomy scale. Nazi
victory awakened them to reality. Women, ignored during
the Kampfzeit, suddenly came to men's attention as they
"normalized" their authority. Before 1933 women had
played a vital, if unrecognized, role in creating a
veneer of goodness and decency which offset the brutal
male élan of the SA. For potential followers, as well
as for party members, women's efforts at social welfare
made the Nazi movement appear to be almost a subculture
- complete with fanatical idealism, self-sacrifice,
righteousness, and community spirit. After the party
stabilized its political dominance, women lost the last
illusions of autonomy and became raw material for propaganda which glorified the decency of a brutal and re-
pressive state. Of course, men in the party experienced
parallel changes, but they typically received bureaucratic sinecures as compensation - and besides they had
not ever been accustomed to as much autonomy as women
had enjoyed in the "old days." Thus the transformation
from idealism to opportunism affected women Nazis in a
special way.
When the party tolerated, and even needed, autonomous and dynamic local organizers, women enjoyed considerable latitude; after 1933-1935, however, party
leaders recruited women who would provide raw material
for propaganda campaigns to cover Nazi brutality with
the healthy gloss of motherhood.

Kershaw.

NOTES

1. Ian Kershaw, <u>Popular Opinion and Political Dissent in the Third Reich</u> (Oxford: Clarendon, 1983).

2. Hitler and his deputies themselves displayed an extraordinary curiosity about the popular response to Nazi policies. Only when they despaired of achieving results by "conversion," did they resort to coercion.

3. The following recent works examine major shifts in women's economic roles and Nazi men's policies on the "woman question," but largely omit women as actors in or as witnesses to Nazi society: Stefan Bajohr, <u>Die Hälfte der Fabrik</u> (Marburg: Arbeiterbewegung, 1979); <u>Dorothee Klinksiek, Die Frau im NS-Staat</u> (Munich: Institut für Zeitgeschichte, 1982); Michael Kater, <u>Vierteljahrshefte für Zeitgeschichte</u>; Annette Kuhn and Valentine Rothe, <u>Frauen im deutschen Reich</u>, 2 vols. (Düsseldorf: Schwann, 1982); <u>Frauen unterm Hakenkreuz</u> (Berlin: EP 94, Elefanten, 1983); Tim Mason, "Women in Germany, 1925-1940," <u>History Workshop</u> (Issues 1 and 2, 1976); Leila Rupp, <u>Mobilizing Women for War</u> (Princeton: Princeton University Press, 1977); Jill Stephenson, <u>The Nazi Organization of Women</u> (London and Totowa, N.J.: Croom Helm and Barnes Noble, 1980), and <u>Women in Nazi Society</u> (London: Croom Helm, 1975); Rita Thalmann, <u>Etre Femme dans le III Reich</u> (Paris: Lafont, 1982); and Dorte Winkler, <u>Frauenarbeit im 'Dritten Reich'</u> (Hamburg: Hoffman und Campe, 1977).

4. Getrud Baumer, <u>Die Frau im neuen Lebensraum</u> (Berlin: Herbig, 1931); Emma Witte, "Die Frau im Lebensraum des Mannes," <u>Nationalsozialistische Monatshefte</u> IV (1933): 29. Male authors on occasion expressed concern about this development: Josef Rompel, <u>Die Frau im Lebensraum des Mannes</u> (Darmstadt: Ernst Hoffmann, 1932); Joseph Beeking, in <u>Die katholische Frau im Lebensraum von Familie, Volk und Kirche</u> (Freiburg: Jugendwohl, 1934), wrote a chapter entitled, "Die Frau im Lebensraum des Mannes," warning men of impending danger.

5. Women teachers' hostility to the Nazi regime contrasts with male Nazis' enthusiasm for Hitler.

6. Gregor Strasser, in a letter dated 8/12/32, noted the unique nature of Nazi propaganda and stressed the importance of "organizational forms which are not dictated from the conference table, but grow organically out of the necessity of daily struggles and the goals which grow up from underneath." Bundesarchiv Koblenz, NS22/348, "Geleitwort." Hitler noted in <u>Mein Kampf</u>, "the function of propaganda is to attract supporters, the function of organization is to win members."

12
Workers and National Socialism

Mary Nolan

Tim Mason has unquestionably done the pioneering as well as the most comprehensive and provocative research and writing on the working class in Nazi Germany.[1] Yet, this work, as Mason himself has admitted, raises as many questions as it answers. In a review of Mason's work, done five years ago, I noted two areas where this was particularly true.[2] Mason's argument that class and class conflict persisted in the Third Reich was solidly based. But if class could not be eliminated, its character could be changed in fundamental ways. Mason told us too little about how that restructuring occurred and what implications it had. Secondly, Mason neglected cultural issues. But the rapidity and thoroughness of the destruction of the SPD and KPD cultures, the meaning of working-class participation in Nazi mass culture, and the failure of the Social Democrats and Communists to rebuild their traditional cultures after 1945 all cried out for explanation.

How far has recent research helped us answer these questions? I want to explore that by focusing on work covering three broad areas: developments on the shop-floor, women workers, and culture. In looking at each of these themes, I (as well as several of the authors whose work is being reviewed) want to stress an expanded chronological framework. I am increasingly convinced that the crucial restructuring of the labor process, workers' culture, and the working class began in the mid-1920s, not in 1933. Whether it continued along the same lines after 1945 and culminated in the 1950s is a question which I cannot answer but which needs to be raised.

Let us look first at investigations of the shop-floor. Recent works by James Wickham on Frankfurt workers in 1929-1930 and by Uta Stolle on chemical and metal firms in the first third of the twentieth century focus on the relationship between transformations of the labor process and the restructuring of the working class and do so in a perspective extending back well before

1933.[3] Both authors investigate how the social fascist line of the Communist Party could have made sense.
They analyze changes on the shop-floor and in the workers' movement to which social fascism was a response, a
response, they argue, at once plausible and disastrous.
Their work sheds broader light on the restructuring of
the working class prior to 1933 and on the divisions and
weaknesses which that restructuring engendered in workers' organizations and culture.

Wickham analyzes the organization of the working-
class movement, the world of the rank and file militant
in Frankfurt. This world, he argues, was fundamentally
altered between 1923 and 1929. The all important
"quasi-institutions," based on the shop-floor and ser-
ving as the basis of cooperation across party lines and
skill levels, were destroyed by both economic and political forces. On the one hand, economic stabilization
and rationalization led to structural unemployment,
plant closings, deskilling, increased employment of
women and an intensified work pace. On the other hand,
the SPD won control of and demobilized the factory dele-
gate meetings (Betriebsräteversammlungen), a key quasi-
institution in Frankfurt. As a result of these changes,
the working-class movement lost its informal institutional base on the shop-floor. Contacts between Socialist and Communist workers occurred less frequently and
only outside the factories. As quasi-institutions disappeared, the official union, party and cultural organizations became the major, if weak, link between skilled
and unskilled. The working-class movement became dependent on hostile political parties. In this changed institutional context, Wickham argues, social fascism
seemed plausible to the KPD rank and file, but it became
a self-fulfilling prophecy. It drove the SPD to the
right and the KPD into ineffective radicalism. It split
not only working-class parties but also the workers'
movement which no longer had informal institutions to
bind it together.

Stolle's study of Bayer, BASF, and Hoechst reinforces the argument that a fundamental restructuring occurred between 1925 and 1929, which carried significant
consequences for working-class organization and activism. Stolle emphasizes that the reorganization of the
work process was at the heart of the rationalization
movement of the mid and late 1920s. Rationalization
demobilized, disorganized and demoralized workers because it intensified work, worsened working conditions
and increased productivity much more than wages. For
some workers rationalization meant structural unemployment, for others deskilling. For all it meant a wor-
sening of the possibilities of communication and informal organization on the shop-floor. Trade union and
party support and communications networks, which were
rooted in the older organization of work, were thus

eroded by the massive restructuring of the labor process. Stolle suggests as well that in the late 1920s
there was a revival of authoritarian and patriarchal
firm social policies, aimed at tying the worker to the
firm and disciplining him or her. This was evident in
the chemical firms she studies and in Ruhr heavy industrial firms which brought in DINTA (the German Institute
for Technical Education), an organization committed to
developing a new, unpolitical and dependent worker for
the new rationalized work.

My own work in rationalization in Weimar reinforces
the conclusions of Wickham and Stolle.[4] Rationalization, whether it came in the form of plant closings, deskilling, work reorganization and intensification or
mechanization, brought pervasive structural unemployment, changes in the labor markets of different industries, and tremendous fear of unemployment to those
still holding jobs. This fear emerges clearly in inter-
views with workers contained in the Weimar government's
1928-1929 investigations of productivity. And fear outweighed workers' dislike of the new rationalized work
and encouraged resignation rather than protest.

The SPD's response to rationalization further encouraged division and demobilization in the working
class. Party and union leaders praised the idea of
rationalization, although not the consequences or precise market strategies of German capital. They encouraged workers to accept the loss of power on the shop-
floor in return for social policy compensations,
achieved by the party, from above, and without mass
mobilization. The state did grant national unemployment
insurance and binding arbitration in wage disputes,
which represented significant reforms. But the Social
Democrats' strategy discouraged activism, divided the
interests of employed and unemployed workers and was
precarious, for concessions depended on a favorable
economic conjuncture and the political good will of
Catholic politicians and the export sector, not on the
economic or political power of the working class.

In short, the German working class was seriously
restructured, divided and economically and politically
demobilized before the Depression and before the break-
through of the Nazis in 1930. This is key to understanding SPD and KPD policies in late Weimar and to
explaining the weakness of the working class and the
success of the Nazis in neutralizing it after 1933.

The most interesting research on the restructuring
of the working class during the Third Reich is Tilla
Siegel's recent study of wage policy.[5] Siegel traces
the results of a wage policy in which the state tried to
set the maximum wage level while the determination of
the wage form reverted to the unilateral control of the
firm. Her argument emphasizes the systematic and pervasive differentiation of wages among skill levels and

occupations and between men and women. Wage increases came in the form of bonuses, special additions and the like, so as to individualize wage differentials and destroy a community of interests among workers. This practice also served to discipline workers and increase productivity. In addition, there were efforts to undermine pay by qualification and to tie wages directly to the activity performed at the work place. Siegel concludes that the differentiation and resulting "neutralization" of the working class was greater than Mason has asserted. Moreover, high pay for some might have been as much an effort to differentiate workers and increase productivity as a concession to thwart worker protest. This very suggestive work raises two important issues. Did these processes begin in the 1920s or were they discussed and planned for by capital then? How much did the practices of the Nazi era set the pattern for post-1945 developments?

Recent scholarship has been more sensitive to the issues raised by feminist scholars than earlier work was, but general discussions of transformations of the labor process and politics still tend to be written from the perspective of male workers, often skilled ones. We thus need to ask explicitly how working-class women were affected by the restructuring of the labor process and the working class in the 1920s and whether National Socialism altered their situation.

It has frequently been assumed that women in Nazi Germany were pushed out of the paid labor force and relegated to the realm of Kinder, Küche and Kirche (children, kitchen, and church). Although these assumptions reflect Nazi rhetoric and capture significant aspects of middle-class women's experiences, they must be greatly modified to grasp the reality of working-class women's lives.

One of the most interesting and provocative contributions to the growing body of literature on women workers is Annemarie Tröger's "Die Frau im wesengemässen Einsatz."[6] Tröger argues that the Nazi era was important in the development of the modern sexual division of labor in waged work and between production and reproduction. In a much more thoroughgoing manner than previous German governments or states elsewhere, the Nazi regime intervened to redefine and to demarcate clearly women's and men's work after the confusion and blurring of the sexual division of labor due to World War I and the rationalization of the 1920s. The aim of Nazi policy, Tröger claims, was not to eliminate women's industrial work by forcing women into the home or relegating them exclusively to agricultural work and domestic service. Rather it was to provide cheap, dequalified labor for industry. Working-class women were to do factory work when young and single, then retreat to the home to have children, only to return again to the factory when

older. Propaganda, job counseling and training as well
as youth programs were all geared to socialize working-
class women to these varied roles.

Tröger is persuasive in showing not only the persistence of women's industrial work but also Nazi acceptance of it. Indeed, she could have elaborated her argument. Carola Sachse's work on Sozialarbeiterinnen -
women welfare workers in factories - shows that the Women's Office of the German Labor Front not only accepted
women's industrial work but hoped to improve attitudes
toward it.[7] Women welfare workers were to instill in
women industrial workers a new work ethic and pride. If
possible, they were to encourage political involvement
and enthusiasm for such policies as eugenics as well.

Tröger is less persuasive in explaining why women's
waged work developed as it did within industry. The
sexual division of labor in industry and between production and reproduction seems to have existed in its 1930s
form already in the mid- and late 1920s. Moreover, the
sexual division of labor developed in a very similar
manner in the United States in the interwar years.
Thus, it is unclear what was new under National Socialism. Stefan Bajohr's empirically rich but analytically
weak study of women textile workers in the late 1920s
suggests significant continuities.[8] Neither the rele-
gation of women to unskilled work and the assembly line,
nor the double burden, nor the lack of time for leisure
and culture, no matter under whose auspices, was new.
It is equally unclear how significant Nazi ideology was
as a causal factor. I suspect it was less a cause of
how and where women worked than an ideological justifi-
cation for a form of women's work that was determined by
capital's need for cheap labor, by the persistence of a
past pattern of the sexual division of labor and by the
absolute economic necessity many working-class women
experienced to do waged work. Neither the dominant Nazi
ideology nor the Labor Front Women's Office variant on
it seems to have had much effect on the work of women
wage laborers, however much Nazism may have altered
their lives and politics in other ways.

My comments on culture will be brief, and, due to
the dearth of work, they will take the form of questions
rather than evaluations of recent work. Mason recently
suggested the need to look at the late 1920s worker's
culture, both Social Democratic and Communist, to see if
it contained elements that promoted working-class integration and a lack of resistance in the Nazi era. The
issue is vital, but we must ask even broader questions
about culture. Virtually no work has been done on the
SPD and KPD culture of the late 1920s and early 1930s.
To understand why that culture was destroyed and the
larger issue of the fate of the working class in the
1930s, we need to examine the extent to which organized
working-class culture had been restructured or had par-

94

tially disintegrated by the late 1920s. What was the
relationship between mass culture and organized working-
class culture - from both the parties' and the individual members' perspectives? Did rationalization disrupt
communities and cultural associations and values just as
it did work and union and party politics? What was the
impact of new attitudes toward sexuality and marriage on
working-class culture? Finally, if, as recent authors
suggest, we need to distinguish between the culture of
the organized workers' movement and a broader working-
class culture, then we need to expand our focus still
further. What was the culture of the unskilled and unorganized? What potential for resistance and integration did it contain before and after 1933? Studies of
culture need to supplement those on work if we are to
understand the fate of German workers in Weimar and
under fascism.

NOTES

1. Timothy W. Mason, Sozialpolitik im Dritten
Reich (Opladen: Westdeutscher Verlag, 1977); "National
Socialism and the Working Class, 1925-May 1933," New
German Critique 11 (1977): 49-93; "Die Bändigung der
Arbeiterklasse im nationalsozialistischen Deutschland,"
in Carola Sachse, Tilla Siegel, Hasso Spode and Wolfgang
Spohn, Angst, Belohnung, Zucht und Ordnung: Herrschafts-
mechanismen im Nationalsozialismus (Opladen: Westdeuts-
cher Verlag, 1982), 11-53.

2. Molly Nolan, "Class Struggles in the Third
Reich," Radical History Review, vol. 4, nos. 2-3
(Spring-Summer 1977): 138-59.

3. James Wickham, "Social Fascism and the Division
of the Working Class Movement: Workers and Political
Parties in the Frankfurt Area 1929-1930," Capital and
Class, no. 7 (Spring 1979): 1-34; Uta Stolle, Arbeiter-
politik im Betrieb: Frauen und Männer, Reformisten und
Radikale, Fach- und Massenarbeiter bei Bayer, BASF,
Bosch und in Solingen (1900-1933) (Frankfurt/Main:
Campus, 1980).

4. Mary Nolan, "Capital, Labor and the State: The
Politics of Rationalization in the Weimar Republic,"
Paper delivered at the American Historical Association
Annual Meeting, December 1981.

5. Tilla Siegel, "Lohnpolitik im national-
sozialistischen Deutschland," in Sachse, Siegel, Spode
and Spohn, 54-139.

6. Annemarie Tröger, "Die Frau im wesensgemässen Einsatz," in Frauengruppe Faschismusforschung, ed., Mutterkreuz und Arbeitsbuch: Zur Geschichte der Frauen in der Weimarer Republik und im Nationalsozialismus (Frankfurt/Main: Fischer, 1981), 246-72.

7. Carola Sachse, "Hausarbeit im Betrieb: Betriebliche Sozialarbeit unter dem Nationalsozialismus," in Sachse, Siegel, Spode and Spohn, 209-94.

8. Stefan Bajohr, Die Hälfte der Fabrik: Geschichte der Frauenarbeit in Deutschland, 1914 bis 1945 (Marburg: Verlag Arbeiterbewegung und Gesellschaftswissenschaft, 1979); Mein Arbeitstag, Mein Wochenende: Berichte von Textilarbeiterinnen (Berlin: Verlag Textilpraxis, n.d.).

13
Organized Mass Culture in the Third Reich: The Women of Kraft durch Freude

Anson Rabinbach

One of the most difficult questions for historians of National Socialism concerns the impact of ideology, particularly on those social groups and individuals that fell outside of loyal and convinced supporters and followers. More specifically I would like to address the problem of the effects of National Socialist mass cultural organizations on those for whom these efforts were directed. In a broader sense I am interested in how intellectual and cultural history can contribute to the question of the degree of "passivity or resistance" by reconceptualizing such issues as the relationship between the politicization of culture and private experience, the relationship between "organized" culture and mass culture, and the determination of cultural choice, cultural reception and "popular" taste.

In order to provide some indication of how this might be achieved I would like to focus on a single document, a 1936 survey of women's participation in Kraft durch Freude (hereafter referred to as 'KdF'), undertaken by the Deutsche Arbeitsfront Frauenamt (DAF).[1] This unpublished survey, entitled "Die Freizeit der Erwerbstätigen Frau," contains detailed information about working women's leisure time activities and preferences in the first three years of Nazi rule. KdF was ostensibly one of the most popular and successful Nazi institutions. Its combination of social policy, ideology and organized mass culture reflected a unique characteristic of the Nazi public sphere. Because it was specifically addressed to men and women workers, to workers and salaried employees, it offers important insights into how working women responded to the range of cultural events and organizations offered, how they perceived the distinction between organized and private leisure activities, and most important, how they chose to define their relationship to the politicized culture of KdF. Finally, the study also identifies a social phenomenon which I think offers a clue to the often hidden reaction of these women to Nazi culture: a pervasive

Lesehunger (the term is from the authors of the study),
a desire for good reading material which demonstrates
the interdependence of politicized, organized mass culture and the pursuit of private cultural interests and
tastes. The act of reading books that are not designed
for indoctrination, reading novels instead of participating in KdF is a social choice, especially within the
limited cultural choices available in the Nazi state.
The pervasive Lesehunger of the KdF women, and, I think
it can be shown, of a large proportion of working and
middle class men and women, offers an important clue to
the ambiguous quality of cultural responses and the
inadequacy of terms such as "integration" or "resistance" in describing them. The results of the study
also make possible some interesting speculations about
the relationship between Nazi organized mass culture,
popular culture and traditional working class culture
which Mary Nolan has noted in her remarks.

Recently, intellectual and cultural history has often been reproached for assuming that the self-image of
the Nazi regime and its reality were identical. Indeed,
in the 1950s and 1960s, historians like George Mosse and
Fritz Stern rejected the view that ideology was simply a
cynical instrument and argued that there was an elective
affinity between pre-1933 traditions of illiberalism and
anti-modernism and the social groups that in moments of
crisis either consciously or unconsciously adopted these
ideas. In the last decade, under the double impact of
the Frankfurt School and the theory of the polycratic
character of the Nazi state the attention of cultural
history has shifted to the disparate components of the
ideological system and the variety of contexts in which
ideology was anchored. This discussion of the National
Socialist "public sphere" (Öffentlichkeit) focused on
the forms and the institutionalization of ideology,
arguing that there was no monolithic "Nazi ideology" but
to some extent a profusion of ideologies tailored for
different cultural and social groups and situations: in
the arts, architecture, music, festivals, rituals,
radio, cinema, the professions, in rural areas and urban
ones. Even more important, the emphasis of this history
on the political dramaturgy of the regime and the use of
"aestheticization" as a means of articulating and rear-
ranging the image of reality, highlighted the unique
character of the Nazi public sphere designed to organize
and absorb private experience into politically useful
forms: in the sports organizations, the Thingspiel movement, the party bookstores and libraries, radio evenings, and of course in the mass tourism and cultural
activities of KdF.

The recent history of everyday life and local and
regional history seems to indicate that this literature
too had overestimated the impact of cultural organizations and ideology.[2] Martin Broszat's multi-author

study of Bavaria, and Ian Kershaw's work on public opinion and the image of Hitler in that province argue that
local resistance was based on traditional attitudes and
local politics, making ideology largely ineffective. At
the same time, however, there was a strong belief in
state authority and a myth of Hitler's infallibility and
personal benevolence.[3] These and other studies of the
social impact of ideology indicate that for those who
were not already believers, there was a widely fluctua-
ting spectrum of attitudes and responses among different
social groups. The problem must be confronted: was
there a deep cleft between the ideology of the Nazi regime (despite its own heterogeneity) and its public reception? What was the impact of the "politicization of
the private sphere?" To what extent did the massive
production of ideology and the creation of so many new
cultural institutions actually impinge on those for whom
it was intended? The KdF study provides some preliminary answers.

In February 1936 the DAF magazine devoted a special
issue to the theme "Die Frau am Werk" (#60) which included a questionnaire asking working women for detailed
information about the amount of leisure time (Freizeit)
available weekly, how they took advantage of KdF, how
they used or preferred to utilize their leisure time and
what occupations afforded greater or lesser "free time."
It also inquired into their preference for private versus public organization of leisure, into how they perceived the KdF cultural offerings, and whether those had
been available to them previously. The response was, as
the authors of the resulting text indicated, unexpected-
ly large (we can assume some pressure from local KdF
women's groups). I should also note that the text is so
obviously critical about the relevance of KdF for women,
and the responses so unenthusiastic, that the study was
never published and received a streng vertraulich status. It is also apparent that the authors, two promi-
nent figures in the Nazi women's organization, Alice
Rilke and Dorothea Goedicke, were aiming at a critical
evaluation that underscored the ambivalence of National
Socialist ideology toward women workers and the difficulties that older, married, and mothering women encoun-
tered in participating in KdF.

The respondents roughly mirror the social composition of KdF (which was an organization of both workers
and white collar employees -an essential part of the
ideology) with 50% mostly clerical employees and 50%
industrial, craft, agricultural and domestic workers.
Membership was generally compulsory. Social access to
leisure time, as reflected in the study, is largely in
accord with the surveys conducted by the trade unions in
Weimar before the crisis: 27% (mostly married women,
single mothers and saleswomen) said that they had absolutely no leisure time.[4] Even single women living

alone complained of little leisure time, at best one-
half to one hour weekly. Younger women, both industrial
and clerical, claimed that they had one to two hours of
leisure time, while the greatest proportion (two to
three hours weekly) fell to the better situated clerical
and white collar employees still living with parents, or
to part-time domestic workers. Women in rural areas
engaged in agricultural and other kinds of work noted
that they had absolutely no time to participate in any
KdF activities.

The success which KdF enjoyed, and on which the
greater part of its propaganda appeal was based, was its
claim to provide German workers access to the cultural
and leisure time activities that were formerly the pri-
vilege of a "small, propertied strata." Modeled on the
Italian Dopolavoro, KdF offered German workers cheap
theater, opera, concert, cabaret and film tickets, cultural evenings and weekends, and the extremely successful travel opportunities ranging from one day outings to
trips to Italy, Norway and Madeira in ships especially
built for mass ocean travel. For 1936, the year of the
study, the most important cultural activities were, in
terms of participation:[5]

Travel (3 days and under)	8.6	(in millions)
Bunte Abende	6.3	
Theater	4.0	
Variety, cabaret	2.5	
Opera, operetta	2.3	
Concerts	1,6	
Film, cinema	1.4	

The women's study reveals that KdF generally made
good on its claims. For example, 36% of the women who
participated in KdF declared that they attended theater
offerings that had not been available to them earlier.
Next to theater, the "short trips, weekends and steamer
tours" were most popular, while only single white collar
workers and a few industrial workers could participate
in the costlier trips to Madeira or Norway (as Hasso
Spöde has shown in detail).[6] An overwhelming 98% of
those that participated in any KdF activity declared
that only through that organization "was the enjoyment
of theater, sports, travel and wandern first made
possible."

A more revealing question was "would you prefer
that in the organization of this leisure time, suggestions be made and choices offered, or would you prefer
to organize your leisure time yourself?" A striking 81%
said that they would prefer to organize it themselves.
This response provoked the authors to add the following
(even more revealing) commentary:

It would be mistaken to see in this very high
figure a corresponding rejection of leisure time
organization such as that offered by the KdF.
Apparently the question was misunderstood by most
of the respondents and it appears that they feared
that someone wanted to "organize" their free time.

But they also conceded that "the formulation of the
question and the kind of response it provoked is extremely interesting psychologically. It shows people's
general need to have a part of their lives over which
they find themselves to be completely and solely in control and that is not 'organized' from an external, alien
source." The relatively low overall figure of 25% for
those that took advantage of any KdF activity, and the
many responses expressing the sentiment that "I am happy
when I have my peace" made the same point.
The results of the study point clearly to a preference for private rather than organized leisure. Only
25% of the women polled preferred to spend their leisure
time in the theater. Movies were also "astonishingly
seldom mentioned." Public music events (concerts and
operas) were also rarely considered, but, "in contrast
the enjoyment of their own music making was relatively
frequent (singing, piano, mandolin, guitar, etc.)."
Apart from the interest in sports and gymnastics among
those under 30, the vast majority preferred to spend
their leisure at home: 37% mentioned "regular sewing and
knitting" (though not repair work), equally divided between workers and employees. Large numbers also spoke
of the need for "fresh air" and "a walk" (27%) or the
"need for sleep and rest." Unlike the Weimar leisure
studies of working women, group activities were conspi-
cuously absent from the responses.
But for my purposes, the most significant finding
of the study is the "remarkably large need for books"
and for reading which was noted in 32.3% of the responses. It was not limited to any specific status, occupation, or age. There was consistent reference to "good"
books, and the authors of the study emphasized that "it
is amazing how often the reading of history books or
books about nature were mentioned." They concluded by
noting that "if you consider that the group addressed is
to a great extent composed of uneducated employees and
workers...the proportion of 'lesehungrigen' women is
very large" (remarking that the "possibilities of influencing and educating them were greatest through the
book"). The study clearly shows that for women in KdF
the organizational benefits were vastly outweighed by
the primacy of the private over the public organization
of leisure time, of which Lesehunger is one manifestation.

THE POLYTECHNIC
WOLVERHAMPTON
FACULTY OF EDUCATION
DUDLEY.

Lesehunger represents, as I think the study demonstrates, a reaction to the perpetual presence of organized cultural activities and the norm of participation.
Even if this phenomenon tells us little about the political "beliefs" of the women of KdF, it tells us about
their attitude towards politics and the intense desire
for a private depoliticized experience. Lesehunger is a
statement about what, under conditions of dictatorship,
represents the utopian side of privatization, a wish or
hope, rather than a conviction. As one of the letters
appended to the study notes:

> (Stenotypist) "...If I had enough time, I would
> just like to read a beautiful book to the end in
> peace. I would just like to be able to converse in
> a circle of good friends, not always with the same
> ones that one works with all day. For this reason
> the evenings with colleagues and factory gatherings
> (Kameradschaftsabende and Betriebsveranstaltungen)
> are not always particularly desirable. I would
> rather just find one possibility to be alone in
> peaceful contemplation, or to take the hand of a
> small child with whom I could laugh or go walking."

The issues raised by these responses bring us to
and important point of intersection between cultural and
social history: in the KdF study we can see the interdependence of the politicization of the private from
above and the privatization of leisure as a reaction to
its politicization. For the cultural historian this
raises a whole gamut of questions about who read what,
when and above all, how -some of which might be addressed with regard to the study.
But it should also be noted that Lesehunger was not
simply or solely limited to KdF. Figures on reading
habits in the Third Reich indicate that there was a pre-
cipitous decline of both working class and bourgeois
reading of "political" and "social" literature in the
Third Reich, while at the same time women showed a
marked preference for "good literature," men for technical books, and all readers showed a growing interest
in works of history in those years.[7] By looking at
those books that were popular and desired apart from
those works for which there was a constant over-supply
(works of political indoctrination and favored authors)
we find that, for example, one of the greatest hits of
the Third Reich was Margaret Mitchell's enormously successful American Civil War epic Vom Winde Verweht sell-
ing almost as many copies as the all-time bestselling
Nazi novel, Hans Zöberlein's Glaube an Deutschland.[8]
The extraordinary success of foreign literature in
translation in general, and the loosening of restric-
tions on undesirable and entertainment (Schmutz und
Schund) literature (including pornography) in the late

1930s and early 1940s also gives some indication of the
regime's eventual recognition that political literature
had not satisfied public taste. Eventually, even the
ban (leveled because of their preference for Scotland
Yard over the bumbling Sicherheitsdienst) on the detec-
tive novels of Dorothy Sayers and Agatha Christie was
lifted. Perhaps Lesehunger can be in part explained by
the National Socialist's knack for choking off the
availability of lower quality "good" literature through
the National Socialist Schriftumspolitik, creating a
desire for works of higher literary quality.

We can also speculate about whether Lesehunger is a
sign of the exhaustion of ideology by 1936-1937, of a
growing recognition that political legitimacy, secured
at the outset by propaganda and terror, had given way to
quiescence. One interesting point of Jean Pierre Faye's
study of the "narrative economy" of the Third Reich is
that the self-contradictory and antinomic character of
the ideological system as whole, characterized by such
combinations as conservative and revolutionary appeals;
corporatist and statist language; national and socialist
rhetoric, volkisch and technocratic (modernist) appeals,
terror and utopia, created a withdrawal from ideology at
all levels.[9] These contradictions caused (this is my
conjecture) an inevitable short-circuit and a flight
into either myth (Kershaw's Führer myth) or into the
private sphere of Verinnerlichung, the family and the
word. The decline in membership of the Hitler Youth,
the waning popularity of mass events, the marginaliza-
tion of the ideologues like Feder and Rosenberg, the
withdrawal of the alte Kämpfer, the official end to the
ritual drama movement (Thingspielbewegung) in 1936, the
withdrawal of the socalled volunteer work for the Bund
deutsche Mädel, Schönheit der Arbeit and KdF, and perhaps even the growing reliance on foreign policy for
approval, were all symptomatic of this rapid de-ideolo-
gization that occurred in the same period as the KdF
study was done.

The ambivalence of Lesehunger is that it can be
read both as evidence of the National Socialist inability to control successfully the production, distribution
and reception of ideology and as the successful channel-
ing of self-expression into a sphere of personal satis-
faction. This brings us back to the issue of how is
ideology effective? Even if it was not always directly
effective (a naive assumption anyway) sometimes it is
indirectly powerful - as form - in this case the intense
politicization of organized culture from above creating
a structural opposition to the ritualized practices of
the Nazi public sphere, as well as to its "steered" and
controlled literary market.

A choice for private as opposed to organized culture is a response to the hegemonic claims of Nazi in-
stitutionalism. But it is also unpolitical in the sense

of "inner freedom" in the face of external authority.
Lesehunger expresses the ambivalent desire of many Germans (as one young writer of those years described his
own feelings) to find a "seligen Reich der Mitte zwischen Alltag und völliger Entrücktheit" in the mid-
1930s.[10] It demonstrates the power of ideology in the
classical sense by embodying in emotionally meaningful
form the real dilemma of those, like the KdF women, who
were neither enthusiasts nor linked to the traditions of
the political labor movement: the inability to find a
political space or mode of expression between the demands of those in power and the demands of conscience.

NOTES

1. Bundesarchiv Koblenz, Deutsche Arbeitsfront,
NS5I 3/4, "Die Freizeit der erwerbstätigen Frau. Ein
Beitrag zur Gegenwartslage der Arbeiterinnen und Ange-
stellten." Ergebnisse einer Umfrage des Frauenamtes der
Deutschen Arbeitsfront an die erwerbstätigen Frauen.
Zusammengestellt und bearbeitet von Alice Rilke und
Dorothea Goedicke. Typescript, 29. All subsequent
quotations not otherwise indicated refer to this
document.

2. For a survey of this literature see Thomas Ber-
ger, "Nationalsozialistischer Alltag," Sozialwissen-
schaftliche Information für Unterricht und Studium, vol.
11, no. 4 (October, 1982): 250-256; Detlev Peukert and
Jürgen Reulecke, eds., Die Reihen fast geschlossen:
Beiträge zur Geschichte des Alltags unterm Nationalsozialismus (Wuppertal: Hammer, 1981); and the discussion
between Jürgen Kocka and Martin Broszat in Merkur:
Deutsche Zeitschrift für europäisches Denken, vol. 36,
no. 10 (October, 1982): 955-65; vol. 36, no. 12
(December, 1982): 1244-1248.

3. Martin Broszat et al., eds. Bayern in der
NS-Zeit (Munich: Oldenbourg, 1977); Ian Kershaw, Der
Hitler-Mythos (Deutsche Verlagsanstalt, 1980).

4. Compare, for example: Susanne Suhr, Die
weiblichen Angestellten: Arbeits- und Lebensver-
hältnisse: Eine Umfrage des Zentralverbandes der
Angestellten (Berlin: Deutscher Textilverband, 1930);
Mein Arbeitstag, Mein Wochenende (Berlin: Deutscher
Textilverband, 1930).

5. Otto Marrenbach, Fundamente des Sieges: Die
Gesamtarbeit der Deutschen Arbeitsfront von 1933 bis

1940 (Berlin: Grundlagen Sozialordnung, 1940), 335;
Hasso Spode, "'Der Deutsche Arbeiter reist'," in Gerhard
Huck, ed., Sozialgeschichte der Freizeit (Wuppertal:
Hammer, 1982), 295.

6. Hasso Spode, "Arbeiterurlaub im Dritten Reich,"
in Carola Sachse, Tila Siegel, Hasso Spode, and Wolfgang
Spohn, Angst, Belohnung, Zucht und Ordnung: Herrschafts-
mechanismus im Nationalsozialismus (Opladen:
Westdeutscher Verlag, 1982), 275-328.

7. Erich Thiers, Gestaltwandel des Arbeiters im
Spiegel seiner Lektüre: Ein Beitrag zur Volkskunde und
Leseführung (Leipzig: n.p., 1939), 76, 112.

8. Dietrich Strothmann, Nationalsozialistische
Literaturpolitik: Ein Beitrag zur Publizistik im Dritten
Reich (Bonn: n.p., 1960), 380-81.

9. Jean Pierre Faye, Langages totalitaires: critique de la raison/l'economie narrative (Paris: Hermann,
1972).

10. "A hallowed central realm between everyday life
and total other-worldliness": cited in Hans Dieter
Schäfter, Das gespaltene Bewusstsein: Deutsche Kultur
und Lebenswirklichkeit 1933-1945 (Munich: n.p., 1981),
23.

14
Workers' Opposition in Nazi Germany: Recent West German Research

Klaus Tenfelde

The following observations are not intended as an
adequate survey of different working class attitudes
towards the Nazi regime, nor of the growing research on
the subject. I want rather to contribute some very
broad remarks in the light of investigations carried out
partly in a small Bavarian miners' town, and partly in
the Ruhr region where I have been focusing on certain
relations between organized resistance on the one hand
and everyday working-class life on the other.[1]
     As is well known by now, most recent West German
research on the history of National Socialism has tended
to broaden its scope by concentrating on aspects of
everyday life (Alltag).[2] This has meant trying to
clarify, among other things, the concrete effects of the
Nazi's crude encroachment upon social life within different strata of the society at different times, and the
response of the people affected. Clearly these aims
seemed best attained by a great number of local and
regional studies in the tradition of William Sheridan
Allen and others; Ian Kershaw's book on popular opinion
and political dissent in Bavaria might be the most recent example.[3] To a growing extent, studies like
these tried to combine methods of social and political
history. Increasingly, they proceeded from description
of the economic and demographic settings to detailed
analysis of the material conditions of life at the work
place, within the social organization of the plant, and
within families, neighborhoods and communities. Smaller
communities have received a lot of attention because it
seemed possible to expliciate the social reasoning of
political behavior especially well in small groups.[4]
     By now it seems to me that research of the kind
described above has led, first, to at least a partial
rejection of the old notion of a totalitarian society
divided between hard-headed, persuaded people, that is,
the overwhelming majority, and the very few who pre-
served a degree of freedom of thought and who organized
against the party and government system on one ground or

another. This is not to deny that the regime generated
its cruel pressure within all fields of social life, a
pressure which constantly compelled people to make up
their minds. But the degree and kind of pressure differed from place to place and from social group to
social group; and so did the popular response. I shall
shortly give some examples.

From my remarks it is also clear that research of
this kind would lead, secondly, to at least a partial
revision of the notion of resistance. This reassessment
has been attempted especially by the research conducted
in Bavaria under the guidance of the Institut für Zeitgeschichte in Munich.[5] There have been serious efforts to redefine the idea of resistance, replacing it
or complementing it by notions such as popular or collective opposition, denial, or Resistenz, the latter
being untranslatable because in English Widerstand and
Resistenz would mean the same. What is meant by Resistenz could perhaps be described as a certain ability to
refrain from the regime's temptations, at least in part,
and usually on the grounds of personal and collective
interests or traditions, family and group relations.
Resistenz has also been applied to cross-cutting loyalties, for example the local Catholic church counsellor
who, although a party member, supported the priest's
supervision of the young people in the local parish,
even as he enrolled his son in the Hitlerjugend. Examples of behavior like this even within the party hierarchy are numerous, not to mention among ordinary people
who, by virtue of some concessions to the regime, sought
to preserve some inviolable aspects of their lives.

Yet to me it seems impossible to renounce a clearly
defined notion of resistance.[6] One should avoid de-
picting a society of fighters against the Nazis by
broadening the scope of resistance. The latter should
be understood to comprehend a real act - or the refusal
to behave as clearly expected - based on an objective
that is contrary to the system's ideological, political
or administrative aims. Genuine resistance should entail a risk of life or liberty; and it should usually be
accompanied by a certain degree of organization.

A clear-cut definition such as this would help to
distinguish the different possibilities of behavior
towards the system that are below the threshold of
resistance as defined above. It is this behavioral
approach that I would like to stress.[7] The mining
community offers a good example for analyzing different
possibilities of behavior within one stratum of the
society. At this point I do not want to recall the
theoretical and methodological literature on the community approach,[8] nor do I want to quote the many
studies exemplifying this approach. Let me just stress
the fact that miners' communities are usually characterized by close connections between the work place, the

mine, and the network of families and neighborhoods with their cohesive material conditions, customs and traditions. These "pure" communities tend to consist almost exclusively of miners, with only a small middle class of petty bourgeoisie and white collar workers, and an almost total absence of an upper class.

Given such a set of conditions one might distinguish some different features of behavior towards the Nazis: First, up to the middle of 1932 the degree of conformity with the Nazi Party's aims was, according to election results and party membership, at least moderately low and usually extremely low.[9] In communities that also had workers, say, in steel mills and in metallurgical plants, electoral support ranged from five to ten percent below the average, while in pure mining communities the Nazis scored even lower. Of course, this is not to say that it was the non-miners who accounted for the better Nazi results in mixed communities; on the contrary, a higher degree of occupational diversification would account for the comparatively good Nazi score, and in that case the miners would probably play their part, but we lack sufficiently disaggregated studies. At the very least, we can observe that pure miners' communities turned out an extremely poor Nazi vote, especially if they were of Catholic confession and also had, as was often the case, a strong Communist tradition.[10] In both cases, the Nazi vote derived from the middle class, and among them white collar workers and the supervisory personnel of the mines, many of whom had changed their politics several times during the last years of the war and the time of the revolution, finally swinging from the left to the right during the inflation or, at the latest, after 1930.

Second, from the July and November elections of 1932 to the March elections of 1933 there was a certain left-wing to right-wing fluctuation which still awaits detailed analysis and which is best shown by the results of the work council elections in March 1933. While the Nazis stopped these nationwide elections because of an obviously wretched outcome for the Nazi unions (NSBO) of about 12 percent, in mixed mining districts the Nazi vote increased to about 30 percent, while the Communists, being outlawed and under strong pressure, lost at about the same rate. The most important cause for this shift, I believe, lies in the fact that at this time the NSBO still appeared to be a union which deserved some support in light of its radical attitudes towards the employers. Yet the partial shift to the Nazis had not yet taken place within the pure mining communities where old loyalties remained strong, so that the Nazis, to take a Southern Bavarian example,[11] scored about 16 percent at the Reichstag elections of March 1933, as compared with 43 to 44 percent in Bavaria

as a whole. The same seems to be true in the northern
parts of the Ruhr region, whereas the southern districts, and especially the ones dominated by a Protestant population and also highly diversified in terms of
occupational structure, scored a much higher Nazi vote.
Given this information, it is easier to understand the
developments from 1933 on.

Third, and speaking generally, the degree of conformity in pure mining communities remained low
throughout the 1930s, while mixed communities might have
been more compliant. In some places, especially in
small, isolated, industrial towns of southern Germany of
Catholic confession, the Nazis met ostensible distrust
of one or the other kind. In work council elections,
now called Vertrauensratswahlen and based on the 1934
Nazi labor legislation, the Gesetz zur Ordnung der
nationalen Arbeit, workers sometimes decided to honor
the last of the list with their vote, and the few vot-
ings in the 1930s show a comparatively high marginal
vote of disagreement. This is also true in the case of
the Ruhr mines, [12] where the Nazi candidates received
such meager support that the Party stopped council
elections after 1935. In such places the NSDAP also had
difficulty building its local party subculture, and the
party carefully refrained from encroachments in plant
and productive matters. On the other hand, plant
officials of the Deutsche Arbeitsfront (DAF) sometimes
successfully struggled to gain the workers' trust at
least to a certain extent, which could be shown, for
instance, in the case of judical advice by the DAF. One
also has to take into account the changing economic
situation which gave, when unemployment ceased from
about 1936 on, some bargaining power back to the
workers. From then on, spontaneous strikes could happen, though strictly forbidden, and, as Tim Mason has
shown,[13] workers increasingly met production pressures
by fluctuation.

No doubt that the relative success of the economic
policy of the Nazis, and also their performance in terms
of foreign policy, led a considerable amount of the working force to change their minds. Yet, as a whole, the
degree of conformity in miners' communities remained
comparatively low. Thus it could be shown, for
instance, that children's participation in the Hitler
Youth was approved by no more than about 50 percent of
parents, though no one could become an apprentice without being a member of the Hitler Youth.

In light of what has been said, one might be
surprised at the fact that organized and ideologically
led resistance remained feeble in communities. The
Nazis met popular opposition, but this did not necessarily mean that sentiments could be purposefully combined for the sake of collective, underground action.
The main reason for this weakness seems to lie in the

simple fact that it was difficult to conceal things where people had known each other for decades.

The opposite was true insofar as workers' communities in large industrial districts like the Ruhr region are concerned. Whereas the popular sentiments of industrial workers did not differ markedly from that in pure mining communities, there were more opportunities to combine popular opposition with active underground work. Real resistance promised more success in large industrial areas, where people could hide and where their efforts could reach many other people.[14] Furthermore, old and well-known local, or even regional, labor leaders were still around, if they had managed to escape from the police terror and legalize their existence on unsuspicious grounds. Some of them, such as Fritz Husemann, the leader of the former miners' union in Bochum, demonstratively showed themselves on the streets.[15]

Fourth, with respect both to general, working-class sentiments about the system and to organized resistance, one ought to distinguish the plant from the community, and different phases of development. But I cannot explore this now in any detail;[16] I prefer to stress one last point.

Fifth, what I stated in general terms at the beginning was also true in the case of workers, and especially the miners: the normal situation was not to work against the Nazis, or to work in favor of them; it was normal to keep oneself somewhere in between. Once one decided to have one's son join the Hitlerjugend, or one's daughter join the Bund deutsche Mädel, then life became safer, even if former left-wing commitments were well known. The ones who had the luck to return from Schutzhaft and concentration camps usually kept their mouths shut and by doing this they enjoyed a better chance to regain work and a fairly decent standard of life after 1935 or 1936. Also, in workers' communities, there might have been a certain amount of agreement between lower party officials and unorganized workers to keep life going, to meet in a sort of hidden understanding for each others' troubles. Recent explorations of popular behavior through oral history have shown numerous examples of attitudes like these.[17] This is not to ignore that there was a considerable, and growing, number of hard-core National Socialists among workers, too. I rather want to stress that among workers it was more normal to get along in life by giving something, for instance becoming a member of one of the party's affiliated organizations, and saving the rest. After all, the Nazis were capable of destroying the political culture of the workers, but they failed to penetrate wholly their class culture, that is, their network of relations, sentiments and values, not the least because that network was rebuilt every day.

NOTES

1. Klaus Tenfelde, Proletarische Provinz:
Radikalisierung und Widerstand in Penzberg/Oberbayern
1900-1945, 2nd ed. (Munich: Oldenbourg, 1982); also the
manuscript articles, "Zur Sozialgeschichte der Arbeiterbewegung im Ruhrgebiet 1918 bis 1933;" "Bergbau und
Nationalsozialismus;" and "Bergarbeiterbewegung und
Widerstand im Nationalsozialismus." These manuscripts
are scheduled for forthcoming publication.

2. See, for example the books by Harold Focke und
Uwe Reimer, Alltag unterm Hankenkreuz: Wie die Nazis des
Leben der Deutschen veränderten. Ein aufklärendes
Lesebuch (Reinbek: Rowohlt, 1979), and Alltag der
Entrechteten. Wie die Nazis mit ihren Gegnern umgingen
(Reinbek: Rowohlt, 1980); also Johannes Beck et al.
eds., Terror und Hoffnung in Deutschland 1933-1945.
Leben im Faschismus (Reinbek: Rowohlt, 1980); with a
typical bias on bibliographical aspects: Sabine Asgodom,
ed., "Halts Maul - sonst kommst nach Dachau!" Frauen
und Männer aus der Arbeiterbewegung berichten über
Widerstand und Verfolgung unter dem Nationalsozialismus
(Cologne: Bund, 1983); see especially the collection of
essays, edited by Detlev Peukert and Jürgen Reulecke,
Die Reihen fast geschlossen. Beiträge zur Geschichte des
Alltags unterm Nationalsozialismus (Wuppertal: Hammer,
1981).

3. Ian Kershaw, Popular Opinion and Political
Dissent in the Third Reich (Oxford: Clarendon, 1983).

4. As an example out of a bulk of literature, see
Bernd Burkhardt, Eine Stadt wird braun: Die nationalsozialistische Machtergreifung in der schwäbischen
Provinz (Hamburg: Hoffmann und Campe, 1980), with
typically misleading implications of everyday history.
In his postscript, Burkhardt maintains, for instance,
that it was everyday life in the German countryside out
of which Hitler came to power ("Es war der Alltag der
deutschen Provinz, aus dem heraus Hitler zur Macht
gelangte," 152). This is to ignore what has to be
learned from the political and economic history of the
Weimar Republic.

5. Meanwhile the well-known research project
sponsored by the Bavarian Ministry for Cultural Affairs
has been completed and is available: Martin Broszat, et
al., eds., Bayern in der NS-Zeit, 6 vols. (Munich:
Oldenbourg, 1977-1983).

6. See Günther Weisenborn, Der lautlose Aufstand:
Bericht über die Widerstandsbewegung des deutschen
Volkes 1933-1945 (re-edited Frankfurt/Main: Röderberg,

1974), 26-28; and especially preface by Broszat in
Bayern in der NS-Zeit vol. II, xviii; also Peter
Hüttenberger, "Vorüberlegungen zum
'Widerstandsbegriff'", in Jürgen Kocka, ed., Theorien in
der Praxis des Historikers (Göttingen: Vandenhoeck,
1977), 117-139; compare also note 14, below.

7. Up to now, there are few examples of
"behavioral history" within the scope of recent German
social history. See Broszat as quoted in note 5, and
the fascinating study by Elke Fröhlich, "Die Heraus-
forderung des Einzelnen," in Bayern in der NS-Zeit, vol.
VI.

8. M.I.A. Bulmer, "Sociological Models of the
Mining Community," Sociological Review 23 (1975): 61-91.

9. See Brian Lee Peterson, The Social Bases of
Working-Class Politics in the Weimar Republic: The
Reichstag Election of December 1924 (University of
Wisconsin dissertation, 1976); Wilfried Böhnke, Die
NSDAP im Ruhrgebiet 1920-1933 (Bonn-Bad Godesberg: Neue
Gesellschaft, 1974); as an illuminating example, Günter
Plum, Gesellschaftsstruktur und politisches Bewusstsein
in einer katholischen Region 1928-1933 (Stuttgart:
Deutsche Verlagsanstalt, 1972): Max H. Kele, Nazis and
Workers: National Socialist Appeals to German Labor,
1919-1933 (Chapel Hill: University of North Carolina
Press, 1972); for a discussion of the literature in more
detail, Tenfelde, Proletarische Provinz, 199-203.

10. Plum, Gesellschaftsstruktur, 31f., and
Tenfelde, Proletarische Provinz, 203; for a contrary
opinion see Peterson, Social Bases, 4 and passim.

11. Tenfelde, Proletarische Provinz, 191f.

12. Ibid., 320-24, and especially Klaus Wisotzky,
Der Ruhrbergbau im Dritten Reich. Studien zur
Sozialpolitik im Ruhrbergbau und zum sozialen Verhalten
der Bergleute in den Jahren 1933 bis 1939 (Düsseldorf:
Schwann, 1983), 273-81: results of work council elec-
tions on various Ruhr mines 1934-35.

13. Tim Mason, Arbeiterklasse und Volks-
gemeinschaft: Dokumente und Materialien zur deutschen
Arbeiterpolitik 1936-1939 (Düsseldorf: Droste, 1975);
see also his "Arbeiteropposition im nationalsozialistischen Deutschland," in Peukert and Reulecke, eds., Die
Reihen, 293-313, and Detlev Peukert, "Arbeiterwider-
stand - Formen und Wirkungsmöglichkeiten," in
Widerstand und Exil der deutschen Arbeiterbewegung
1933-1945 (Bonn: Neue Gesellschaft, 1981), 215-364
(including documents).

14. See especially Detlev Peukert's studies: Ruhrarbeiter gegen den Faschismus: Dokumentation über den Widerstand im Ruhrgebiet 1933-1945 (Wuppertal: Hammer, 1980) Volksgenossen und Gemeinschaftsfremde. Anspassung, Ausmerze und Aufbegehren unter dem National-sozialismus (Cologne: Bund, 1982); also Richard Löwenthal and Patrik von zur Mühlen, eds., Widerstand und Verweigerung in Deutschland 1933 bis 1945 (Bonn: Dietz, 1982).

15. August Schmidt, Lang war der Weg (Bochum: IG Bergbau, 1958), 212-14.

16. See the books cited in note 14, and the more conventional studies such as Kurt Klotzbach, Gegen den Nationalsozialismus. Widerstand und Verfolgung in Dortmund 1930-1945. Eine historisch-politische Studie (Hanover: Verlag für Literatur und Zeitgeschehen, 1969).

17. Lutz Niethammer, ed., "Die Jahre weiss man nicht, wo man die heute hinsetzen soll": Faschismus-erfahrungen im Ruhrgebiet (Berlin/Bonn: Dietz, 1983).

15
Discussion

Discussion Chair Peter Jelavich outlined four
general issues that he felt informed the presentations
of Klaus Tenfelde, Anson Rabinbach, Mary Nolan and
Claudia Koonz. First, Jelavich pointed to questions on
the notion of resistance to the Nazi regime within Germany. Second, Jelavich raised the question of how the
historian measures Nazi success, if the Nazis are indeed
understood to be "fighting over souls," and not merely
working for economic recovery, rearmament, or victory in
war. Third, and in a related vein, Jelavich noted the
problem of understanding Nazi ideology, this task being
a central concern if Nazi success is "about ideas."
Finally, Jelavich noted the attempt to situate the as-
cendance of the NSDAP within broader trends from the
1920s to the 1950s, especially the decay of autonomous
structures in a modernizing, rationalizing society.
Klemens von Klemperer addressed the question of
Widerstand and Resistenz, noting that there was not very
much of the former up to 1935. Von Klemperer stated
that the term Resistenz is awkward. It represents a
preliminary to actual Widerstand (translated as the more
familiar "resistance"). Resistenz is a way of "staving
off the total intrusion of Nazi dominion, and of salvag-
ing a minimum amount of pluralism; it's a rear-guard
action," von Klemperer said.
Von Klemperer said that the reason for the dearth
of actual Widerstand is clear: those who were likely to
resist were up against a strong Nazi consensus. This
contrasted with the situation in occupied countries,
where there was some measure of social support for resistance. Von Klemperer also noted that resistance in
Germany was initiated by workers, but was broken down by
the terror of the Nazis. All that remained in the early
years was a "resistance of individuals;" one must recall, von Klemperer said, that "in Germany, not even the
name Widerstand existed, or was used, at the time."
Von Klemperer sought to place these observations
within a wider context, however, and pointed out that
resistance was small and late in all countries, as in

Germany, with the possible exception of Holland. Von Klemperer also asserted that in no country did resistance "go out of existing social groups."

In this line of thought, von Klemperer commented on the conference as a whole, "perhaps we have excessively concerned ourselves with existing social classes and types, even when it comes to the people who were Nazis." Von Klemperer suggested that emphasis be placed on the motivations of individuals, and that what Peter Hüttenberger terms the "representation" theory ought to be de-emphasized in turn. In Germany, the resistance contained "all kinds of strange bedfellows": the resistance did not come out of existing institutions, such as the army, the church, or the bureaucracy, but, rather, what resistance there was coalesced from individuals with different motivations.

Joseph Rovan concurred with von Klemperer on the meaning of resistance in France and in Germany. Rovan, himself a member of the resistance movement in France, said that French resisters had an "easier stand" than their German counterparts, for French resisters had a clear enemy, strong external allies, and a real hope of success. Resistance in Germany, without these things, Rovan commented, was only "for the sake of mankind."

In comparing resistance movements, William Sheridan Allen noted that the Communist and Socialist underground in Germany indeed had a clear goal, that is, the revolutionary overthrow of Hitler. But, these groups were exposed to "uncompromising" terror in the first years, Allen said. In the later years, family connections were the only ones strong enough to maintain resistance. Under the pressure of state terror the underground was further weakened by an "undercurrent of apathy...drunkenness...despair."

Allen also commented on Tenfelde's presentation of resistance. Allen maintained that the regime encouraged ritualistic accommodation, and left inner attitudes alone, especially after 1935. The main reason for this, Allen said, was "simple exhaustion." A second factor was the changing of the guard: the so-called "oldfighters" being replaced by the Märzgefallene (the post-1933 adherents).

On workers' resistance, Hans Mommsen noted that initial efforts among steel and coal workers took place when the workers' families were split. The first stage was when workers were asked to take their meals in the factories, and when women and children were to be moved out of urban areas. In general, however, there was little resistance, Mommsen said, save that of the Communists and some other small groups.

David Abraham noted a "distinct parallel" between the evolution of the debate on integration and resistance, and the debate on intentionalism and functionalism. Abraham traced the development of thought on re-

sistance from the work of Franz Neumann, which stressed
support for the regime by the exploited, to works in
which "anything and everything" was considered some form
of resistance, to the current suggestion that a good
part of the population "sat it out." Abraham saw this
as a move from condemnation to complication and ambiguity, and asked what moral or historiographical perspective this new position implied.

Jeff Weintraub posed three questions for the analysis of authoritarian states: First, to what extent does
a regime destroy the possibility for organized resistance? Second, to what extent can a regime overcome the
"built-in inertia of ordinary social life?" by which
Weintraub meant the combination of "associative networks
outside organized political activity" together with the
simple "exhaustion" that afflicts political organizations themselves. And third, to what extent can a
regime "actually stimulate real enthusiasm or active
support?"

Weintraub used the examples of Italy, Germany and
the Soviet Union to illustrate comparisons based on the
above questions. The Italians, Weintraub said, neither
destroyed resistance, nor controlled social life, nor
even enjoyed popularity. Both the German and the Soviet
regimes destroyed bases for opposition. The Soviets,
Weintraub noted, did more to attack groups outside organized political activity. Weintraub said, however,
that the Nazis were much more successful, at least up to
the invasion of the Soviet Union, in generating real
support: "the Nazi regime was much more popular" than
the Soviet regime. Weintraub closed by querying why
the Nazi regime enjoyed such popularity, acquiescence
and activity.

Erich Goldhagen proposed that the decisive difference between Germany and the Soviet Union was the ideological pluralism of the Nazi regime. The "social
strength" of the regime derived from the fact that
people were able to pick and choose among the various
facets of Nazism. Goldhagen remarked that:

> the regime succeeded in striking deep roots in the
> vast majority of the population who accepted frag-
> ments of their ideology and anchored themselves by
> means of these fragments to the regime. There were
> only a few islands of total rejection. And these
> were people who were imbued with a counter-ideo-
> logy: the only ones were the Socialists and Commu-
> nists, they were totally immune to this, no element
> of Nazi ideology could penetrate their conscious-
> ness.

Tenfelde, in his summary remarks, offered several
conditions necessary for Resistenz (or denial) to become
full Widerstand (or resistance) in Germany. First, a

location in a big city, or cluster of big cities, was
necessary. Second, Tenfelde said that a geographical
proximity to free countries was essential. This was
exemplified for Tenfelde by those German cities close to
the Low Countries: internal German resistance dropped in
1940 when the Nazis crossed the border. Finally, Tenfelde noted the importance of a network of group relations, persons, and personal qualities. Tenfelde
maintained that resistance grew out of existing social
groups. Concurring with Rovan, Tenfelde said that the
objective of resistance, especially during the years
1933-1939, was difficult to discern. In this regard,
Tenfelde offered the example of Franz Foucht, the leading Social Democrat in the Ruhr miners' resistance, who
committed suicide and left his colleagues with a "strong
feeling of despair and apathy."
        Tenfelde also agreed with Allen's comment that a
change of attitude in the NSDAP took place in 1935, as
exhaustion set in. Before 1935 "was the time when the
party system was clean, so to say; the party itself, and
also the DAF (German Labor Front), was clean of former
functionaries and so on." After 1935, the important
details of party operations, such as collection of
money, suffered neglect.
        Several participants directed their comments to
Nazi culture and the privatization of individual life as
had been discussed by Anson Rabinbach. Mommsen noted a
tendency of the regime itself to depoliticize private
life. Mommsen also registered a certain skepticism
about the existence of Nazi culture, stating that, as an
amalgam, it did not constitute a culture of its own.
Jeffrey Herf asked whether the turn to the private
sphere was something new, or in fact was a part of the
German tradition of disinterest in politics.
        Dan White asked if there is "a way of measuring
what enthusiasm is," and doubted the historian's ability
to employ meaningfully terms such as privatization.
Tenfelde rejoined that privatization could be observed
in patterns of church attendance, as he noted von Klemperer had done. Tenfelde also suggested that one could
measure the Lesehunger (avidity to read) that Rabinbach
had described, and contrast it with what the regime said
at the outset in 1933-1934: "don't read too much, it
just makes you corrupt."
        In his final remarks, Rabinbach reiterated that
there was a demand to participate in Nazi culture on the
part of Germans, and underscored his position that there
was indeed a Nazi culture. But, Rabinbach noted, "it is
really extraordinary how little we know about simple
things like reading habits of different social groups in
the Third Reich." Rabinbach said that readership of war
novels, contrary to their supposed popularity, declined
"precipitously exactly in 1933," just as the regime
began producing them. Rabinbach also said that "scien-

tific works of the ideological variety" also declined in readership. Rabinbach stated that only two percent of "racial novels" in the Leipziger Volksbibliothek were checked out by workers, the rest were charged to academics. Without a study of these phenomena, Rabinbach concluded, we will not know why the regime produced so much popular culture, or what its impact was.

On the issue of women and the Nazi party, Michael Kater maintained that the later amalgamation of women into the Nazi fold was not unique. The same was true, Kater said, of other groups before 1933, including students, youth, doctors and other professional groupings.

Kater also stated that the "quasi-emancipatory dogma or ideology" of Nazi women was missing in the presentations. Claudia Koonz concurred that early women Nazis were fighters for what they perceived to be women's rights, but noted that they became disillusioned after 1933, because of what Koonz labeled "unrealistic expectations." Mary Nolan added that there was a quasi-emancipatory ideology on the labor front. It was, Nolan said, an ideology that did not appeal to women with the "double burden" of work at home and wage labor. When firms ran welfare programs, Nolan mentioned as an example, the programs tended to be geared towards the families of workers, not towards women workers themselves.

Thomas Childers argued that though the Nazis did ignore women in the organizational sense, they paid a great deal of attention to women in the elections of 1932. "In fact," Childers said, "of all of the different occupational and demographic groups that the Nazis attempted to reach in 1932, women were the primary target of the propaganda coming out of Berlin and Munich." Childers outlined the two dominant themes in propaganda directed towards women: the first was to respond to charges from the conservatives and the bourgeois parties that the NSDAP was opposed to the church; the second was to respond to charges from Communist parties that the NSDAP sought to put women out of work. Childers noted that this second charge was a difficult one for the Nazis to answer, for they also attempted to make a great deal out of "anti-feminist notions of women in the work-place." The Nazis argued that it was "inevitable" that some women would have to work, such as unmarried women, but their key point was that women were, in effect, "objects of capitalist exploitation, and that the liberation of women under the Weimar Republic had done nothing but enslave women." Childers closed with the remark that it remained to be explained why there was a "surge" of women voters after 1932.

Koonz, in her final comments, sought to explain that surge. Koonz said that the major objection to the Nazis most women felt was religious, so propaganda breaking down the notion that Nazis were anti-religious resulted in a large body of support. The ranks of Pro-

testant women voters were in disarray two years later,
for the expectation fostered by this propaganda was
false (just as was the hope fostered by suggestion of a
quasi-emancipatory program).

Koonz also argued that women's ideology was critical first for their mobilization and then for their
political demobilization after 1932. Their biggest
complaint, for example,

> was that they did not get enough to read, they did
> not get enough indoctrination school, they did not
> have the tools with which to fight the intellectual
> battle....Ideology for them, access to doctrine,
> was the equivalent to reading their own Bibles and
> interpreting them, and it seemed to give these
> women access to power.

Finally, Koonz said, ideology provided the irrational
axioms for their world view; from these axioms they
derived logical conclusions. From the axiom that Jews
were not people, Koonz noted, it followed "logically"
that they were aesthetically undesirable. Koonz hoped
in this way to account for the "combination of irrationality and logic in the thinking of Nazi people."

Andrei Markovits asked Mary Nolan to clarify the
concept of rationalization she had employed in her presentation. Markovits suggested that rationalization as
modernization took place over a long time, thus implying
that the 1920s were not as crucial as Nolan had argued.
Markovits queried what it was about that decade that
made for changes in the composition of the labor force
and new patterns of relations between the labor force
and machines. Markovits maintained that the crucial
changes of that decade occurred not in the realm of
economics, but in that of politics. The SPD made a
trade-off of "shop-floor power for statist power,"
leading to a "desolidarization of the working class,"
Markovits said.

In a different manner, Herf also suggested that the
decade of the 1920s did not have the significance Nolan
assigned to it. Herf noted that the processes Nolan
outlined also took place in the United States. The
most important difference between Germany and the United
States, Herf said, was the presence or absence of a
dictator. This, and not rationalization, was the decisive factor in working class politics and culture,
Herf concluded.

Nolan, in her closing remarks, said that she employed the term "rationalization" as it was used in
Germany at the time, to refer to a wide range of processes associated with a "restructuring" of the economy.
Nolan underscored the importance of studying these phenomena, for they were linked to the downfall to two
strong workers' movements, the Communists and the So-

cialists. Nolan reiterated her belief that these events
"cannot be explained solely by dictatorship and terror."
    Michael Geyer stated that the industrialization
that took place during the war served as the basis for
the economic boom under the Federal Republic. Geyer
added that a significant degree of rationalization was
associated with this development. Klaus Tenfelde rejoined that the industrialization of the countryside was
an important achievement of the Nazis, but was confined
largely to the south of Germany.

16
Variety in Perception:
Western Views of Nazi Germany

Edward W. Bennett

In this paper, I wish to consider the Western reaction to the Nazi regime as a problem in Verstehen or
understanding. By understanding, I mean not imaginative
sympathy or empathy, but comprehension of another's intent. Also, I mean not primarily comprehension on the
part of historians, but comprehension between the people
in history.
For understanding is practiced, whether well or
poorly, by everybody. Max Weber recognized this when he
defined social action as "that action which, in the
sense intended by the actor or actors, is related to,
and oriented in its execution toward, the behavior of
others."[1] As Weber showed, the understanding people
in society have of each other can be a matter for his-
torial or sociological study.
From a Weberian's viewpoint, the normal functioning
of a given society or culture depends on communication
or understanding. Historians, though, are often especially interested in those situations in which things
are not functioning well. The fact that each society,
even group, has its own channels and forms of communication is, in itself, a source of malfunction, since
there are many societies or groups, and to belong to one
is to be an outsider for others. It seems to be that
history can be illuminated if we pay more attention to
the frequent absence of understanding between people,
especially between people who belong to different
groups. Differences in language, culture, religion, or
ideology obstruct understanding. So also with physical
distance and class distance, from continent to continent
or from ghetto to suburb. The result is an absence of
the open, uncoerced discussion that can lead to genuine
consensus.[2] Competition between cultures or groups
fosters communication within each of them and discour-
ages it between them. And many failures in communication arise from people's attention being diverted in
different directions, having each a different focus.
All this might perhaps be called "ethnomisunderstand-

ing." The influence of misunderstanding on events may
seem elementary and obvious, but by the very nature of
misunderstanding, we are seldom aware that it is taking
place. Thus, for example, we seldom realize that those
people who seem to us to be in the wrong almost
invariably believe themselves to be in the right.

The isolation of national communities from each
other is an especially potent source of misunderstanding. Each has its own culture and often its own language, also its own past (which is much the same thing
as its culture). We read our own newspapers. If we
speak of "the economy," it is our national one. The
nation is the largest group that we naturally refer to
as "we." Most people in such a society are guided by a
persisting conventional wisdom. They see things in the
light of the generally accepted interpretation of the
national experience, through national spectacles. The
greatest chance for the acceptance of an innovation may
come when an older order has clearly gone bankrupt - as
with France after the Franco-Prussian War; Germany
after the 1918 defeat, the inflation, the depression;
the United States after the 1929 crash and the 1933 bank
holiday. Even in these cases, though, there will certainly be some elements of the old among the new. A
situation of bankruptcy may even evoke an atavistic
reverence for older ways, or what are thought to be
older ways.

In France, for example, the national experience
fostered a belief in alliances. Lack of alliances had
been one source of defeat in 1870-1871. After that,
France felt herself pretty much at Germany's mercy until
she was able to gain an alliance with Russia and
ententes with Italy and England. French diplomats believed that World War I might have been prevented if the
British had made their support for France clearer, so as
to deter Germany. In any case alliances had saved
France from defeat. After the war, new alliances were
made with the East European successor states, but these
increased French commitments without bringing much
strength. What the French thought they really needed
was firm commitments from Britain and the United States.
Nazi excesses gave them no surprise, and indeed were
almost gratifying in confirming their beliefs about the
German character. The immediate effect of Hitler's
seizure of power was to reinforce the French source for
guarantees. As Britain and the United States refused to
supply them, France tried to get agreements with the
Soviets and Italy, and to reaffirm the East European
alliances. The French pactomanie seemed almost com-
pulsive, like a hypochondriac trying more and different
pills. At the same time, as often pointed out, France
failed to maintain the army appropriate to her policy.

In British eyes, the Great War had been a terrible
and unnecessary departure from the Victorian norm, a

result of arms and automatic alliances. What the French saw as a search for allies and security, the British saw as a dangerous perpetuation of the division of Europe into rival alignments. French reparations policy, the British thought, had clung to a Carthaginian peace; now the French refusal simply to disarm themselves was blocking a more genuine peace settlement. Some British and American policy makers thought that a disarmament of France would actually increase French security. On the other hand, much of British opinion had come by 1933 to sympathize with the German underdog; London hoped to induce the Germans to accept the League, to remain disarmed, and to live in peace and quiet. As the 1930s began, British military strength was much reduces revulsion against war widespread and respectable, and the economy was ailing with little sign of a strong recovery. The dominions were isolationist, and so were many Englishmen.

If Hitler's takeover confirmed French assumptions, it was harder to reconcile with prevailing British conceptions. It is always possible to find arguments to save a theory, however, and the British could blame Hitler's rise on French intransigence. In early 1933, the British had just gotten the Germans back into disarmament discussions, and they could not immediately abandon that enterprise. Similarly, when the British finally had a chance to sign an arms agreement with the Germans - the Anglo-German naval agreement of 1935 - they seized it. It is hard to turn away from a goal one has been committed to, as this amounts to a confession of error. Those in Britain who were most prescient about Hitler were apt to be the old-fashioned nationalists who had no commitment to disarmament to defend.

Americans shared the British repugnance for alliances and the view that war had been avoidable. It seem to them that American participation in World War I had been especially avoidable. But the American reaction to Hitler's takeover was also, and especially, a case where interest was mainly focused or diverted elsewhere. In the 1920s, some aspects of American life, such as Prohibition and restrictive immigration laws, represented a backward-looking attempt to regain simplicity and an idealized past. Americans believed that they had a special and separate destiny. On the other hand, American financial leaders had done much in the 1920s, in what they thought was their own and the world's interest, to prop up the major European economies, German, French, and British. But the German involvement proved unfortunate in 1931, in circumstances that fostered a strong dislike for France. By that time, the United States had already entered into a severe depression which, more than in France or Britain, brought the policies and elites of the '20s into question. A disaster for the capitalist system was com-

parable, for the United States, to a military defeat for
Germany; just as there was a Black Thursday in October
1929 for the New York Stack Exchange. The old business
leadership lost its prestige, and unlike the German general staff, it failed to develop a stab-in-the-back
legend.[3]

After 1932, war debt defaults soured Americans on
France, Britain, and any European entanglements, and the
growing prospect of another European war also strengthened American isolationism. But above all, the domestic
depression was an overwhelming preoccupation. As
American presidents go, Franklin Roosevelt was unusually
informed about European attitudes and affairs, and he
seems to have had few illusions about the Nazis. But at
first he had little time for foreign affairs; he sacrificed international interests that might impinge on
recovery, and he offered no overt resistance to isolationist currents.

German politics and culture were even less compre-
hensible to people in each Western country than the
politics and cultures of the other Western nations were.
In 1931, Heinrich Brüning actually sought a financial
crisis to end the national disgrace of reparations;
American leaders could not conceive of the possibility
of such a policy. Some Western observers thought that
President von Hindenburg might restrain Hitler, or even
that Hitler might restrain the Reichswehr. There was a
theory that Germany could not afford to rearm very much.
Aside from national differences, most respectable
middle-class Westerners had little experience with amor-
al freebooters and ruthless trench-warfare survivors
like the Nazi leaders (or for that matter, the Black and
Tans and Auxiliaries in Ireland). People in the West
also had only a dim sense of the strong national convic-
tions and social and bureaucratic pressures that had
supported German revisionism and rearmament, and that
now helped to silence the doubts of respectable Germans.
In 1933 and 1934, the Nazi treatment of the Jews and the
Röhm purge did give evidence that this was a regime that
had passed beyond the bounds of civilization; unfortunately, the evidence was not sufficiently heeded.

One might argue that, whatever the problems of
understanding or comprehension, far-sighted Western
leaders should have known what to do. The principle of
the balance of power should have dictated Western unity
and preparedness. And actually, almost subconsciously,
natural impulse for group self-defense did begin to make
themselves felt. But British and American observers
tended to hold that the balance of power, as a principle
was outdated, and anyway they believed that the balance
of military force clearly favored the French; belief in
French military strength remained strong up until May
1940. The judgment of the balance of forces may appear
to be an objective, quantifiable matter, but in practice

the assessment is commonly influenced by the case that
the assessor wishes, on other grounds, to make. One can
count (or try to) the number of men under arms, or the
number of tanks, or now, of missiles and warheads, but
the relative value given any particular category is
still a qualitative question. Also, non-material considerations like strategic concepts and tactical doctrines need to be weighed, and military organizations
need to be seen in their historical and social context.
There is an Anglo-American belief that any inference as
to intention is unscientific, subjective, and specula-
tive, and such inferences can indeed be biased. Yet
intention is more crucial than hardware, and information
for a well-founded hypothesis as to intention is sometimes available, at least for those who will pay attention to it, who can translate it, and who can put it
into its context.

Respecting Nazi Germany, such information had in
fact been provided by Hitler himself. Joseph Goebbels
stated in April 1940 that if he (Goebbels) had been the
French premier in 1933, he would have said: "The man who
wrote the book Mein Kampf, in which it says so and so,
has become Chancellor of the Reich. The man cannot be
tolerated in our proximity. Either he disappears, or we
march." Goebbels continued: "That would have been completely logical. They refrained from that. They let us
alone, they let us pass through the danger zone un-
hindered, and we were able to sail past all the reefs,
and when we were ready, well armed, better than they,
they began the war."[4]

Actually, as Goebbels must have known, the Nazis
had tried, with some success, to block the publication
of unabridged translations of Mein Kampf. Through most
of the 1930s only an abridged version was available in
English. An unauthorized complete translation was published in France in 1934, but the Nazi Eher Verlag successfully brought court action to suppress it, on copyright grounds, and even an abridged edition only became
available to the French public in 1938.[5] Of course,
Western foreign offices were presumably competent to
translate the book for official use. But in a democracy
it was not enough for a prime minister to read the book
- it had to be read widely, so as to arouse public
awareness. A French premier would also have needed a
wide British reading of it, so as to gain British support. Indeed, one may wonder how many French or British
readers could conceivably have understood the significance of the work. An understanding of foreign thinking
is not likely to be widespread among the public, or
indeed among leaders who must face a democratic electorate. We readily assume that we understand the thinking
of people of a different culture, yet in practice it is
difficult even to approach such a comprehension. We
must seek it deliberately opening our minds to the per-

spective of the other culture, even though we will not
wish to - and indeed will be unable to - cast off our
own outlook.[6] If one is looking for a reason for
studying history, one such reason would be that the
effort to understand past policies and cultures may
serve (even though in fact it often does not) to sensi-
tize us to the existence of other viewpoints.

If the West was disunited and also slow to understand the Nazi danger, it may be some consolation that
Hitler was even less successful in understanding British
predilections and policy. As Karl Rohe has recently
pointed out. Hitler's dream of an Anglo-German alliance
against the Soviet Union, and perhaps against the United
States and France, never had a chance to materialize,
even though, from the viewpoint of pure Realpolitik,
such an agreement might have made sense to a maker of
British policy.[7] It would be hard to imagine a more
misdirected invitation than that which Hitler, in July
1933, reportedly gave to Arthur Henderson, an upright
Methodist and former Labor Foreign Secretary, who was
then trying to save the Disarmament Conference. Hitler
said: "You know, you have the best fleet in the world,
and we will have the best army in the world. If we
could reach an understanding, you and we, the world
would belong to us."[8] In December 1933, Hitler asked
the British ambassador if Britain might not like to have
alternatives to her existing friendships; in June 1935,
at the negotiations on the Anglo-German naval treaty,
Joachim von Ribbentrop read a statement, almost certainly drawn up with Hitler, that called for a "common
realistic, basic conception on the part of the two countries toward the great European problems."[9]

But the British were deaf to German suggestions of
an alliance and probably did not even realize that such
suggestions had been made. Owing to their whole political and cultural tradition, Western governments had no
common ground with Hitler. Indeed, by the end of 1933,
leaders in all the Western countries were starting to
think - if very reluctantly - of the possible eventu-
ality of war with Germany, even though they continued
for six years to cherish the hope that such a war might
be averted.

NOTES

1. Max Weber, Gesammelte Aufsätze zur
Wissenschaftslehre, 5th ed. (Tübingen: Mohr, 1982),
429.

2. For a recent discussion: Jürgen Habermas, Theorie des kommunikativen Handelns (Frankfurt/Main: Suhrkamp, 1982), I, 44-71.

3. If not a legend, the private economy did eventually find an alibi for the depression when Milton Friedman and Anna Jacobson Schwartz attributed the severity of the crisis to the mistakes of "officials," i.e., central bankers: A Monetary History of the United States, 1867-1960 (Princeton: Princeton University Press, 1963), Chapter 7.

4. Andreas Hillgruber Hitlers Strategie: Politik und Kriegführung 1940-1941 (Frankfurt/Main: Bernard & Graefe 1965), 14, citing Sammlung H.A. Jacobsen, Bonn. Also quote in Hillgruber, Deutschlands Rolle in der Vorgeschichte der beiden Weltkriege (Göttingen: Vandenhoeck & Ruprecht, 1967), 76-7, translated by William C. Kirby as Germany and the Two World Wars (Cambridge, Mass.: Harvard University Press, 1981), 56-7, 103n. Hans-Adolf Jacobsen, Der Zweite Weltkrieg: Grundzüge der Politik und Strategie in Dokumenten (Frankfurt/Main: Fischer, 1965), 180-81, provides other portions of Goebbels' remarks, made on 5 April 1940 to a small group of press representatives. Hillgruber notes a similarity to Hitler's oft-cited comment to his generals, on 3 February 1933, that if France had statesmen, she would assail Germany before the latter could rearm.

5. For a survey of the Anglo-American publishing history: James J. Barnes and Patience P. Barnes, Hitler's "Mein Kampf" in Britain and America: A Publishing History, 1930-193 (Cambridge: Cambridge University Press, 1980). The unauthorized French edition: Adolf Hitler, Mon Combat, translated by S. Gaudefroy-Demombynes and A. Calmettes (Paris: Nouvelles Editions Latines, 1934); a copy is available at the Harvard University Library. The abridged French edition: Adolf Hitler, Ma Doctrine, translated and edited by Francois Danture and Georges Blond (Paris: Fayard, 1938); in this version, Hitler's anti-French remarks are somewhat abbreviated, and are accompanied by conciliatory statements made by the Führer on later occasions. See London Times, 6 March 1934: 13; 5 June 1934: 14; 21 June 1934: 13, for accounts of the Eher lawsuit.

6. Hans-Georg Gadamer has stressed that full understanding of a foreign or past culture is unattainable: Wahrheit und Methode: Grundzüge einer philosophischen Hermeneutik, 3rd ed. (Tübingen: Mohr, 1972), 483-84, 518. On the process of virtual understanding by the historian or social scientist, cf.

130

Habermas, Theorie, I, 165-71, 189-95; Habermas also presented these views at a conference on "Hermeneutics and Critical Theory" at Bryn Mawr College, 19 February 1983.

7. Karl Rohe, "Die Westmächte und das Dritte Reich 1933-1939: Zusammenfassungen - Fragen - Perspektiven," in K. Rohe, ed., Die Westmächte und das Dritte Reich 1933-1939: Klassiche Grossmachtrivalität oder Kampf zwischen Demokratie und Diktatur? (Paderborn: Schöningh, 1982), esp. 185-95.

8. Maurice Vaisse, Sécurité d'abord: La politique française en matière de désarmament, 9 décembre 1930 - 17 avril 1934 (Paris: Editions A. Pedone, 1981), 440, from the unpublished recollections of Thanassis Aghnides in the League of Nations archives.

9. E.L. Woodward et al., eds., Documents on British Foreign Policy, 1919-1939, 2/VI (London: Her Majesty's Stationery Office, 1957), No. 99; Jost Dülffer, Weimar, Hitler und die Marine: Reichspolitik und Flottenbau 1920-1939 (Düsseldorf: Droste, 1973), 325-28.

17
France and Hitler: 1933–1936

Joseph Rovan

The day when Hitler came to power in Germany there was no government in France. One may consider this fact as a pure coincidence, but then it was a very symbolic coincidence. It shows that at the very moment when Germany gave itself to a totalitarian regime, France was entering a phase of important political difficulties; her Republican regime was entering the ultimate phase of decomposition. During the small space of time between the beginning of Nazi reign in Germany and the declaration of war, France consumed eleven governments, and between the fall of one government and the formation of the following there were long periods of transition without real power. All the governments were the result of very precarious parliamentary coalitions, without substantial unity of program, especially in the field of foreign affairs, a field in which all the parties and groups became progressively more and more divided.

In these times the interest in foreign developments and the knowledge of foreign developments were very poor in France. Even among the militants of the left, only a few people understood the importance of the change in Germany; very few had a solid knowledge of Hitler's ideas and intentions. The most important leader of the left, Léon Blum, head of the Socialist Party, shared the illusions of the majority of German democrats before the nomination of Hitler as Chancellor. They did not know much of his program and they thought that his regime could not last a long time. There had been a certain amount of interest, before 1933, in the Italian fascism, even among some important men in the French Socialist Party, interest in an experience which seemed to have restored the power of the state, interest in a kind of third way between capitalism and Marxist socialism. A part of this interest was then slowly transferred to an interest in Nazism. The weakness of the republican state, its inability to deal with the economic crisis, the lack of perspective in Léon Blum's idealistic

leadership and a mixture of personal ambition and of
patriotism, provoked in 1933, some weeks after Hitler's
coming to power, the partition of the old Socialist
Party. Many of the leaders of the new Parti Socialiste
de France became some years later outstanding leaders of
the collaboration with Nazi Germany.

Very gradually and generally, first, among intellectual circles, we must turn to the development of an
anti-fascist feeling and anti-fascist movement. The
sympathy for the refugees from Germany and the growing
information on terror in Germany helped this development, but in the Socialist Party anti-fascism had to
evolve in contradiction to the deep-rooted tradition of
pacifism. The formation of the Front Populaire is due
for the most part, to internal reasons: the growing of
militant extremism from the right, with clearly anti-
democratic and anti-republican objectives. Naturally,
the way things were developing in Germany, and the attempted coup against Dollfuss in Vienna in the summer of
1934, exercised some influence, but the main interest
was internal. During the two years between February 6,
1934, and the formation of Léon Blum's first government,
the socialist group in the House of Deputies continued
to refuse to vote for the defense budget.

The most important external factor was, in fact,
the strategic change in the Communist international
movement, the consequences of which appeared in France
in 1934. The Communist Party stopped its furious attacks against the socialists; Maurice Thorez offered
friendship and alliance to Catholics; and even the very
centrist and bourgeois Radical Party were accepted in
the Front Populaire. The Communist Party was the only
one that was deeply aware of the whole international
implications, but the horizon in which it developed its
allies was not French but Russian. Nevertheless, the
Communist conversion to anti-fascist patriotism established the foundation for what happened in the Resistance after 1941, following the parenthesis of the
Hitler-Stalin pact. In the meantime, the Communist
Party's deputies voted alone, in September, 1938,
against the Munich accords; they were joined by only a
single socialist deputy and a single conservative
deputy.

The new Nazi regime brought also important changes
into the ranks of the right. As was the case on the
left, these changes had a contradictory nature. On one
hand, the traditional anti-German feeling was reinforced
by the coming into power of the German extreme right,
allied to the old nationalists and monarchists. Poin-
caré and Tardieu, the leaders who resisted Briand's policy of reconciliation with Germany, saw their positions
confirmed by the events on the other side of the Rhine:
Hitler's decision on external and defense questions,
his departure from the League of Nations, the Dollfuss

episode, rearmament, and then the German-British agreement on naval rearmament (which also revived the French right's long-standing resentment of the English). All of these developments strengthened the deep-rooted fear of German demographic and material superiority in the old conservative right.

On the other hand, the radical wing of the French right was full of admiration for the way Hitler dealt with a democratic republic, with democratic parties, for his ideology of violence, of nationalism and of anti-Semitism. Very few Catholics were aware, like Robert J. Harcourt, of the deep anti-Christian tendency within National-Socialism. Indeed, the instrumental conception of religion as a servant to the political objectives of this movement, prepared Charles Maurras and many members of the Action Française for a more positive attitude towards Nazism, with whom the Vatican, at the same time, concluded the Concordat.

The moderate and the extremist wings of the right acted, as did the left, mainly as a function of the internal French situation. The weakness of the republican state appeared when the extreme-right leagues won the street battle of the sixth of February, 1934. As a result, the moderate right came to power (with Gaston Doumergue who called Pétain to his government), but the program of restoring a stronger state authority failed, reinforcing the radicalism of the extreme right. Beside the Leagues' separate organizations, there now appeared new groups, such as the Synarchie, which had strong links to fascist Italy; some of these groups entered the field of political murder.

The influence of intellectuals is quite important. Going further than the old-fashioned Action Française, many younger people proclaimed their admiration for Hitler's ideas, his methods, and for the renovation he brought to his nation. The disgust with the corrupt and inefficient old Republic, with its political personnel with long beards and big bellies, was strong even among many of the young Catholics who some years later became a main reservoir for the resistance. As transfusions from the socialist and the Communist parties, together with plebian extremists from the right, built up small, French fascist parties, the radical influence of extreme right-wing papers such as Gringoire, Candide, and Je suis partout grew quickly.

The formation of the Front Populaire raised alarm among the possessors of economic power. The fear of Bolshevism gave birth to a growing sympathy with Hitler's Germany and the deep political influence of organizations such as the Comité des forges was turned towards a policy of non-confrontation with fascist powers. This became of great importance after the outbreak of the Spanish Civil War. The influence of those with economic power on the Radical Party, which was a necessary partner in the Front Populaire majority, was then evident.

Thus, while the majority of the right was for appeasement with Mussolini and Hitler, a minority actually considered themselves as Hitler's allies. The intellectuals of the extreme right became the leaders of an anti-left pacifism, accusing the left of preparing the war in the interest of Hitler's Jewish enemies, and not in the interest of the French nation. Violent campaigns of xenophobia and anti-Semitism exploited the economic crisis and the middle class fear of foreign and specifically Jewish concurrence.

During the same time, militant pacifism made progress in the ranks of the Socialist Party, as well as in the radical-left youth movements, where the influence of the anarchist tradition was very strong. The convergence of these two currents exercised a paralyzing influence on public opinion. France would be unable to react when Hitler sent his army to the left bank of the Rhine, unable to react to the German-Italian military intervention in Spain, unable to react to the Anschluss of Austria. The inability to understand the real nature of the Nazi regime, as well as the growing number of actual allies Hitler found in France, lead France to the defeat of 1940, to the fall of democracy, and to the demise of the Republic.

18
Discussion

The discussion following the presentations of the commentators addressed two main tasks: the evaluation of Neville Chamberlain's appeasement policy, and the explanation for the weak reaction to the Nazi regime by the French government.

Bernard Wasserstein began the discussion by establishing several distinctions designed to defend the presumably realistic advocates of appeasement. First, "there were appeasers and appeasers....there were appeasers who thought in terms of power relationships.... and there were appeasers who thought in terms of the League of Nations Union." Wasserstein then added a second distinction: between the "ins" and the "outs," or the "decision-makers" and the "debators."

Several participants challenged Wasserstein's contentions. Jeff Weintraub said that Wasserstein had not adequately shown how the two cleavages overlapped. Stanley Hoffmann observed that the "hards" included both appeasers and anti-appeasers, as long as they did not favor a League of Nations strategy, and commented that this "makes very little sense." A number of participants mentioned that Winston Churchill had not been categorized by Wasserstein as either an "in" or an "out."

Michael Smith asked how a sympathetic view of appeasement, such as Wasserstein's, could be reconciled with the arguments that were made on behalf of appeasement at the time. Smith contrasted Wasserstein's assertion that appeasers knew they were up against something radically new with an argument E.H. Carr made in the first edition of his The Twenty Years' Crisis:Nineteen Nineteen to Ninety Thirty-Nine (Macmillan: 1939). This argument was excised from later editions. Carr had argued that Germany would adopt the ideology of a satisfied power and hence the status quo morality once other Western states had given in to a certain extent. "The essence of good policy," as Smith paraphrased Carr, "was to give in to them before they were in a position to take it." Smith asserted that this judgment of

Carr's was not compatible with an interpretation of appeasement as a sensible foreign policy.

Smith commented further that the distinctions Wasserstein drew were similar to Arnold Wolfer's distinction between "collectivists" and "traditionalists" in 1940. All the "collectivists" were not appeasers, Smith said, such as Arnold Toynbee and Alfred Zimmerman. These men were opposed to appeasement because it did not apply the principles of the League of Nations. Smith also noted that within the realist appeasers, Wasserstein would include people who were in favor of dealing with Germany easily and those who would apply the balance of power.

Stephen Schuker assumed the burden of revising the analysis of appeasement, but from a different point of view. In a word, Schuker asserted that a calculus of England's national interests, performed by a person with Chamberlain's particular concerns, would lead logically to a policy of appeasing Hitler. In addition, Schuker argued that the French left was in large measure responsible for that country's poor military preparedness. Schuker concluded, moreover, that only hindsight would provide indications that the new German state would behave beyond reasonable expectations in foreign relations.

Schuker's argument in more detail was as follows: Chamberlain, and his view of England, dominated British government from 1931 to 1939. Chamberlain's vision of England was of recovery under private capitalist auspices, once she was off the gold standard and once she enjoyed easy money and a balanced budget. This approach was designed to encourage industry in the home counties and to provide incentives for workers to leave Wales and other depressed areas. Such an approach required significant tariff barriers and, consequently, concessions to the other Commonwealth nations (including a voice in defense and foreign policy). The whole program, according to Schuker, left little room for defense spending.

Chamberlain had the concerns of a "Birmingham businessman who wanted to revive England, as his father had during the tariff campaign of '05," Schuker said. "The logic is: build your empire, keep your defenses to a minimum, and construct your defense force in such a way that it will keep your empire going." That, Schuker maintained, implied a strong navy, a "territorial" army for use in the colonies, and an air force capable of protecting the home islands. Such a strategy called for an army without heavy weapons and an air force composed of short-range bombers.

"If that is your strategy," Schuker continued, "and you have your economic sphere in the empire, why not let Germany have their economic sphere in Eastern Europe?" "Let them have their protected economic sphere," Schuker suggested, "you cannot afford to intervene anyway."

British officials took a "global view," one that
included concerns as distant as Shanghai, Hong Kong and
Australia, said Schuker. "Germany for England is only a
small part of things: if you are going to read only the
C18 files [German political affairs] in the Foreign
Office, you don't get the picture."

When the "scare" about the German air force came in
1935, Schuker said, one reassessed the military situation. But by then the British were up against the
"rationing problem": they did not have enough resources
to build an army, nor were they in a position to be able
to cut the navy, leaving them the only option of
developing a defensive, fighter force.

After developing this view of British interests,
Schuker went on to assert that Chamberlain's view of the
Nazi regime, given the evidence available at the time,
was not deluded. Chamberlain read German, had read Mein
Kampf early and in the original, and was anti-Nazi,
according to Schuker. And after the "brief terror" in
the spring of 1933, Schuker said, "little was heard in
the foreign press about much terror." The "Night of the
Long Knives" was seen as "the elimination of the
irresponsible Nazis, [thus] allowing the moderates like
Hitler to retain their power," Schuker said. "The
Communists and socialists who were in the concentration
camps, the Jews who had left, that stuff was all over in
the spring of '33," Schuker continued, "and indeed in
1934-5 there was substantial Jewish immigration back to
Germany from those who had left for Switzerland and then
said, 'well, it is all over, now the good Nazis are
back...we'll get by.'"

Schuker also asserted that Sir Anthony Eden and
others (not including Chamberlain) were, "for racial
reasons," anti-Italian. The ostensible argument was
that if Italy controlled Abyssinia, they would dominate
the eastern Mediterranean and be en route to India.
Schuker stated that it was a "nonsensical" position, but
one that was articulated nonetheless.

To this view of the situation in England, Schuker
added several comments on the position of France. The
French, Schuker maintained, were aware that the British
were not going to intervene in the Rhineland or Eastern
Europe, and that the British could not intervene if they
wished to do so: "France really had to write off England
as a serious ally...[the French knew that] when you are
making serious military plans, England would not be
there right away." "And indeed," Schuker noted, "in '39
England was not there. England had to pull back troops
from India - the only troops who knew which end of a gun
to shoot - to get their four divisions on the field."

Schuker observed that cuts in French defense
spending fell heavily on research and development, as a
result of the high fixed costs of maintaining universal
service. Schuker described the French army as "museum-

piece planes and tanks, utterly preposterous, it was a
joke; so that France had, much earlier than one thinks,
no army." Schuker commented that the main point of the
Franco-Soviet pact of 1935 was that the Communists in
France would not commit sabotage. This implied that the
only hope left France, on Schuker's view, was the "vain
hope" for an alliance with Mussolini.

Schuker, citing the Léon Blum and Edouard Daladier
files at the Fondation des Sciences Politiques also
argued that Blum and Daladier behaved "badly" with
respect to defense policy. In Schuker's words:

> Daladier...sabotaged the army, he sabotaged the
> program for air-force building, he behaved in the
> most atrocious way, playing to the left wing of the
> radical party against the Herriot faction for
> inner-party reasons; but at least by '36 he knew
> what he was doing, and when he became Minister of
> Defense in '36, far too late...for doing anything
> serious, the first thing he did was to have his
> staff draw up a memorandum on what President
> Daladier has done for national defense. In other
> words, he, in July '36, had a sense that it was
> going to end badly and he was covering his tracks.
> While Blum continued to behave badly for a very
> long time, Daladier became obsessive on the ques-
> tion of Blum. One of the things that Daladier then
> did with the staff at the Ministry of Defense was
> to set people to work, as early as the fall of '36,
> collecting long statements of Léon Blum's attempts
> to sabotage the army early--and you find folder
> after folder of Daladier material on [this], if it
> had come out, it could have been used against Blum
> in the Riom trials...it is actually quite
> powerful....It makes you understand why the people
> at Riom felt that these people had been
> grave-diggers.

Stanley Hoffmann said that "the question remains
whether this particular view of Chamberlain, which I
think Stephen Schuker described extremely well, made any
sense at all." By "sense," Hoffmann said he meant
having an appreciation of "what Hitler Germany was up
to, whether Hitler would be satisfied with merely an
economic sphere in Eastern Europe, and whether this
world vision of British economic recovery [was viable],
concentrating as Stephen Schuker says on the future
problems raised by the United States and Japan, and
essentially forgetting about Germany." Hoffmann added
that the fact that there were others at the time who
disagreed with this view suggests that one may be
critical of it, even without the benefit of hindsight.

Hans Mommsen maintained that it is not "fair" to
charge the British or the French with being unaware of

the real situation, when even Germans, German conservatives, and opponents of the regime - those people "in
the environment of Hitler" - did not believe that
Hitler's policies would lead to European war. Moreover,
Mommsen said, "a lot of things did not make 'sense'" at
that time.

What were the alternatives? What could have been
done? Any German government would have been subjected
to strong nationalist demands to repeal certain portions
of the Versailles Treaty, Mommsen said; it is therefore
very difficult to say to the British government that it
should have prevented the concessions they made Hitler,
which, in other conditions, if there had been a German
general as dictator for instance, would have been the
correct ones.

Hoffmann rejoined that people at the time discerned
the real nature of the Nazi regime, including foreign
diplomats who reported back to their capitals. "The
proof of the pudding," Hoffmann said, "was in the
eating."

Hoffmann also maintained that in France, even in
Republican circles and among such "bastions of the
regime" as Guidolphe Sey,

> there is the sense of impotence, of being caught
> between a clear writing on the wall and the impos-
> sible general and geo-political and domestic situa-
> tion; the sense of a complete discrepancy between
> the situation in which one is and the means one
> has....That leads, with very, very few exceptions
> to a kind of open-eyed abdication, of which the
> most characteristic was Daladier, who knew exactly
> what he was doing and did it, and essentially was
> lucid; while Chamberlain, I think was not lucid, in
> the sense that he knew that Munich was not exactly
> a gain either for honor or peace in our time.

With regard to Chamberlain, David Abraham said that "in
the land of the blind, the one-eyed man is Prime Minister."
Abraham also argued that Chamberlain would have gone further
towards appeasement than his colleagues, noting Chamberlain
was willing to offer Central Africa, not only Central Europe, to the Germans in February of 1938.

Saul Friedländer asked Schuker how his conception would
explain changes in British policy at certain points.
Neither Britain nor France moved when Hitler went West, into
the Rhineland, but only when he moved East; what, Friedländer asked, was the consideration that prompted this?

Charles Maier concurred with Schuker that formulating
policy based on a reading of another government's intent is
indeed a problematic approach to decision-making. But Maier
urged Schuker to push his revision of British foreign
policy, with its renunciation of the continental counterweight, through to the end. Chamberlain, Maier argued,

"reacted emotionally in March of 1939, he felt that he had
been double-crossed." Maier noted that while French military capability did "lag," German military forces up through
1936 were "derisory in comparison with anything that the
French could muster. After all, the German government had
fallen in December of 1932 over the threat that the Poles
might march in while there was a domestic insurrection [in
Germany]."

"What is striking," Maier noted, "is the inability, the
unwillingness...to credit what strength Paris or London
could bring to bear....at various stages there are options
for freedom of action." This is not to say that the British
and the French failed to understand Mein Kampf in a crucial
way, any more than American policy-makers are to be faulted
for a misreading of the Communist Manifesto, Maier
cautioned. The issue, Maier said, is at every state of the
line determining what is the possible range of German outcomes, what Germany as a real power is likely to do, and
what counter-actions make sense. Maier concluded that the
historian's

> quarrel with the appeasers would not be that they
> didn't read Mein Kampf, or that they didn't take it
> seriously, but that at various points they, in a
> sense, believed that they had much more limited
> options than they might have had; and, as in the
> case of Chamberlain, they outlined a type of policy
> which...was far more utopian in some ways in pre-
> serving British power than standing up to Germany
> would have been.

Schuker rejoined that the West was unprepared for
war at the time of the Munich talks, that Chamberlain
was right to put off the war in 1938 and 1939, and that
Chamberlain was correct in commenting that "Hitler
missed the bus." It became apparent that Hitler had
indeed "missed the bus" when England managed to win the
Battle of Britain "by about four weeks of production
line," Schuker said.

Schuker noted that when Chamberlain became Prime
Minister, he was not in a position to fire Eden, "not
having caught him in enough lies." It was not until
December 1937, when Austin Chamberlain's widow went to
Italy, that Chamberlain learned that Eden had been pro-
viding false information on Mussolini's intentions.
That is when Chamberlain saw the turn coming and fired
Eden. Munich itself represented no great change,
though, as there was no chance of war at all: "in Sep-
tember 1930 it is all newspaper stuff," Schuker said.

"The whole idea that they could go to war at Munich
is nonsense." Schuker illustrated this contention by
relating a September 1938 meeting Chamberlain called
with several newspaper editors (including such writers
as Liddel Hart of the Times) who were agitating for

military action. Chamberlain informed them that the
anti-aircraft guns placed in Hyde Park, the only type
capable of defending against Germany's high-altitude
bombers, would not in fact be supplied with suitable am-
munition until January of 1939. "The guns were put
there to fool German intelligence: there is no anti-
aircraft at all."

Schuker maintained that a similar situation
pertained in France, "no one in France possibly
contemplated going to war at Munich; when you see the
mobilization reports you realize that they cribbed
general mobilization and nobody went. And the people
who had the keys to the offices to bring out stuff,
didn't come."

Chamberlain, Schuker asserted, never changed his
mind; up until 1940, he was always willing to go to a
certain point, but no further. Chamberlain was prepared
to accept border changes in Eastern Europe, dominance of
Eastern Europe and dominance of Central Africa. If,
however, Hitler is out for world domination, "then
there's no ball game," Schuker said. Chamberlain
offered the same deal, Schuker argued, up to the
invasion of Scandinavia, "so that looking at 1939-40
will show the consistency of Chamberlain's policy." "In
any case," Schuker said, "Chamberlain believed by 1938
the longer you could put off the war, the better Britain
would come out, because they needed time to build their
fighter air force." The idea that "Hitler missed the
bus" has a good deal of appeal to it, Schuker concluded.

MacGregor Knox stated that the idea that the West
was at a military disadvantage at Munich is "complete
nonsense," citing for support Williamson Murray's work,
The Change in the European Balance of Power, 1938-1939:
The Path to Ruin (Princeton University Press, 1984).
Knox also said that the assessment of another government's intentions "is the responsibility of political
leadership, that is what people are there for in power."

Knox stated that a crucial difference between
Chamberlain and Churchill was their appreciation of
defense matters: Churchill "had a fascination with
military affairs and technique, which none of the other
people in the government had, and this left him uniquely
able to make an accurate assessment of the military
consequences of Nazi lack of 'gentlemanliness.'" The
1939 Cabinet discussions on what to do with Italy were
"completely puerile," but "once Churchill gets in the
Cabinet things change: the Chief of Staff cannot pull
the wool over the eyes of the politicians."

Edward Bennett commented that the material in the
Cabinet files, especially the Cabinet conclusions, "does
not show a great perception of the character of the
Hitler regime," although the opposite impression could
be gleaned from the Foreign Office files. Bennett also
noted that there was a strong League of Nations element

in the Foreign Office, at least up until 1934. Bennett
said that a series of British proposals, such as the
MacDonald Plan, which attempted to save the idea of
rearmament, were largely a "political wash," for "no
politician could turn his back on disarmament."

Bennett argued that Chamberlain did shift his
position in 1939 in accord with balance of power
considerations. "This may have been more politics on
his part than balance of power thinking," Bennett said,
"but a reaction of the whole British public which he had
to take account of...is the practical working of the
balance of power." Bennett acknowledged the depth of
Schuker's research, but cautioned that a Western politician, in reacting to Mein Kampf, Hitler, and the Nazi
state, "had to take account of the state of public opinion in his country and, for that matter, in the other
Western countries."

Michael Smith, offering a final comment on the
British stance, noted that there are two sorts of
revisionism: First, one could argue that there was a
"positive side to appeasement," that it was not "simply
giving in on every point." Second, one could maintain
that appeasement was "a kind of sensible and coherent
policy." Smith said that Schuker had presented a strong
case for the first, but that several key points undermined the second. Chamberlain's own assessment of
Hitler, in the letters to his sisters, was dangerously
naive. Chamberlain personally hated Nazism, Smith said,
but he had no appreciation for the unique character of
the regime. Moreover, Smith commented, there was the
"extraordinary capacity for continued self-deception and
the sheer vanity of the man: he refused simply to admit
that he was wrong about Hitler when it became very clear
that he was wrong."

Mommsen asked to what extent the perception of
Hitler as a leader surrounded by more radical elements
in his party persisted among the diplomatic community.
David Kaiser answered that there was no doubt that
Henderson saw things as the German conservatives did,
in terms of moderates and extremists within the German
government. Kaiser cited a telegram from Sir Nevile
Henderson (the British Ambassador to Germany) which
Kaiser paraphrased to read, "on the one hand the extremists are pushing, on the other hand we have the
moderates, of which I believe Hitler in his saner
moments is."

Mommsen also asked for a clarification of the connection between the head of the SA, Ernst Röhm, and the
former Chancellor, General Kurt von Schleicher and
French diplomats before the events of June 1934.
Mommsen noted that some letters of Brüning indicate that
there was indeed some communication on the matter.
Edward Bennett answered that though he had little trust
in Brüning's sources, or his ability to report accurate-

ly in the first place, there is nonetheless some sub-
stantiation for his comment. André Tardieu believed in
1934, when the question of drawing up the April 17 note
was under discussion, that the regime would not last
long. This was one of André Tardieu's arguments for a
strong note, Bennett said. Joseph Rovan said that he
had never seen any evidence of the French trying to get
in touch with Röhm. French conservative ministers,
moreover, would have preferred Hitler to Röhm anyway,
Rovan said.

Rovan also stated that more arguments on the problem of the French left are possible. In 1933, after
Hitler's coming to power, the French Socialist part, for
the first time, planned to vote for the defense budget.
Indeed, eighty-nine members of the Socialist group voted
in favor, but Blum himself abstained with thirty others,
and ten more refused to vote. Another year later, Rovan
noted, all returned to opposition. But against these
observations was the fact that Marshal Henri Pétain and
General Maurin were Ministers of War from 1934 to 1936.
Rather than the French left alone, Rovan said, "the real
problem is the incapacity of making an even normal defense policy after 1931, it was a common situation for
different reasons, as well of the left as of the right."
Rovan explained that

> there had been a kind of progress in demoralization
> in the French general situation, and this is also
> why the <u>union</u> <u>sacrée</u> was no longer possible.
> ...Contrary to the situation before 1914, this time
> in the French right, [there was] the feeling that
> they could not avoid in the next years the coming
> of the socialists to government....[There was also]
> the long reflection that the periodic outbreak of
> civil war situations in France came in this time to
> a new climax.

Rovan underlined the importance of the "civil war" problem in comparing the domestic situation of France with
that of Britain, for there was no danger of civil war in
Britain, while those in France and those in the Resistance "were preparing for it."

Why did the French not come when Hitler
remilitarized the Rhineland? The Head-of-Staff told the
Prime Minister that to match thirty-thousand Germans
entering the Rhineland, Rovan said, a general mobilization was necessary. "This is not a problem of material incapacity," Rovan said, "we had forces enough to
match thirty-thousand Germans coming with very small
armaments; it was a kind of moral disarmament, because
it was not true that we needed to make a general mobilization." "Moral factors," the "incapacity of matching a
situation out of internal difficulties," and the "feeling that nobody could really act as having a national

consensus, as finally they had in 1914," together accounted for the French behavior, Rovan concluded.

Rovan addressed another issue, the "biological im-
possibility for France to stand a new war of the kind of
the First." Without being conscious of it, France
nevertheless acted in a manner which averted an outcome
which would have cost it two million deaths, and would
have meant the end of the French nation. Instead, Rovan
said, France lost only 500,000 lives:

> Nobody decided individually to act like this; you
> understood it in the common idea which was so
> strong in France at the end of the war, that Pétain
> and DeGaulle were acting together, and finally, it
> was not true from the real matter of fact, but in a
> superior way, it was true, there was a kind of
> division of war between both of them, which finally
> made the best of a tremendous situation for the
> French nation.

Discussion Chair Stanley Hoffmann ended the discussion with a comment on the tendency to overestimate
Italy and Germany before their time. Hoffmann registered concern over attempts to justify "the inevitable,"
noting that there are often alternatives available to
historical actors.

19
A Roundtable Discussion

The place of Nazism in history, indeed, its place
in social theory generally, occupied the participants in
the final, round table discussion. Nazism defied cate-
gorization for some historians: Saul Friedländer, for
example, rejected the notion that the Nazi phenomenon
falls under such headings as Germanism, fascism or
totalitarianism. Similarly, Richard Hamilton underlined
his skepticism about the usefulness of viewing the rise
of the Third Reich as a product of class interests and
class struggle. For other historians, the difficulty of
situating Nazism in social theory did not lessen the importance of the endeavor: Charles Maier reiterated the
role of comparisons in the study of history; Juan Linz
offered a fresh look at the relation between Nazism and
Fascism, one that accounted for the problems raised by
Friedländer and others; and David Abraham argued that
social and economic groups in Weimar, notably the business class, indeed had a say in the collapse of the
Republic.

Naturally, several debates that had commenced in
preceding sessions were recalled in this closing context. The SPD and the relevance of various critiques of
its strategy concerned Mary Nolan and David Abraham. In
the same manner, Nolan and Hamilton again took up the
suggestion that the collapse of Weimar could be seen as
a crisis of the welfare state. The roles of ideology
and of anti-Semitism were addressed by most of the commentators, notably by Friedländer, Herf, Childers,
Caplan, and Kater. An understanding of relations
between the Führer, his deputies and the masses also
informed the comments of several participants.

Saul Friedländer, adopting the position that racial
theories were at the core of Nazism, argued that neither
Germanism, nor fascism, nor totalitarianism account for
Nazism. Friedländer noted that Germany's nineteenth
century völkisch racism was not unique, for French culture had many similar ideas, as documented by Zeëv
Sternhell.[1] Friedländer also noted Richard Levy's

observation that anti-Semitic parties disappeared in
Germany on the eve of World War I.[2] A rise in anti-
Semitism did take place during World War I, with 1916 as
turning point, but anti-Semitism went down again after
1923. And anti-Semitism was not a theme in the campaigns of the early 1930s, Friedländer said. Furthermore, Friedländer continued, public opinion polls at the
time showed that Germans were not much taken by anti-
Semitic notions. Anti-Semitism and anti-Semitic ideas
ought not be seen as progressing in a linear or self-
sustaining process, concluded Friedländer, rather, anti-
Semitic ideology "went through small channels into small
groups and into the party...into sections of the party."
    Friedländer rejected attempts to incorporate anti-
Semitism within a theory of fascism, as Ernst Nolte,
Hans Mommsen and Wolfgang Schieder had tried to do.[3]
Nolte's Three Faces of Fascism cast anti-Semitism as the
radical anti-Bolshevism of the extreme fascists. But.
countered Friedländer, Hitler's early writings devote
far more attention to Jews than to Communists. Anti-
Semitism nurtured anti-Bolshevism, not the other way
around. Mommsen had argued that the structure of fascist parties, not their ideology, caused radicalization.
Friedländer argued that structure alone was not enough
to account for radicalization: the case of Italy, in
which the Italian Grand Council threw Mussolini out in
1943, showed that cumulative moderation could also
result from fascist structure.[4] Friedländer finally
cautioned against Schieder's equation of Nazi anti-
-Semitism with xenophobic, racist ideas in other countries. Friedländer questioned Schieder's thesis that
the effect of the war is an adequate explanation for the
differences between Nazi anti-Semitism and Italian
racism.
    In the end, Friedländer suggested that no theory
had adequately explained Nazism. The Nazi regime could
be conceived of only as a hybrid of the three dominant
characterizations - Germanism. fascism and totalitarianism. And to these three, Friedländer concluded, one
also had to add the element of Hitler himself.
    Maier asserted that historians need theory, even if
theories fall short of accounting for historical complexity. Historians make comparisons, Maier said, and
they create theory by doing so. Maier agreed with
Friedländer's downplaying of a continuing "Germanic
ideology" as the root of Nazism, but noted that there
are other continuities to look for, such as those in
party structure, bureaucracy and economic interests.
Maier did note with caution that theory could be exploited to serve political purposes. On the one hand,
"Fascismustheorie" (the prevailing Marxian explanation
that links Nazism and other fascisms as a capitalist
dictatorial recourse) had been widely condemned at the
Berlin conference of January 1983[5] because of the

theory's connection to the left and its popularity in
the late 1960s. On the other hand, Maier said, even
stressing anti-Semitism as the central element of Nazism
could be exploited politically. One understood, for
instance, that East Germans had claimed that their
society bore no residual guilt for Nazism, since Nazism
had been the product of another and now transcended
social system, namely capitalism. By stressing radical
anti-Semitism as the hallmark of Nazism, West German
commentators seemed more willing to own up to its horrible elements and its uniquely German character. In
reality, Maier feared, by so emphasizing genocidal anti-
Semitism and not other aspects, these historians themselves sealed off the Third Reich from the continuities
of German history. West Germans allegedly confronted
the most horrible aspect of Nazism, but in fact
distanced themselves from it.

Taking the perspective of a visitor from the moon,
Maier proposed, "some things about the human experience
occurring after the Great War...cry out to be seen as a
group." Maier suggested, first, that an examination of
decision-making in Germany, Italy and Russia would be a
fruitful comparison. Second, Maier suggested that one
might construct a formal theory of administrative
"chaos" in states with strong personalities, where controlling access to the leader was crucial, offering the
unlikely comparison of Hitler and Roosevelt. Third,
Maier proposed a contrast in the use of terror in Russia
(stochastic, unpredictable, designed to make everyone a
possible victim) with its use in Germany (applied to
specific groups, predictable, designed to draw a line
between the secure and the outsider).

Fascism, Maier concluded, could be seen as an answer to certain historical burdens: military defeat or a
frustrated victory, an organized, Marxist-inspired working class that seemed to overwhelm bourgeois elements, a
weak parliament, and pre-liberal political patterns.
Germany and Italy were similar in these respects, but if
the man from the moon were to look at the period after
the installation of these regimes, Maier said, he might
bracket Stalinism and Hitlerism together instead. Fascism makes sense as a concept to respond to questions
about prior history; for questions about the regimes,
the idea of totalitarianism is a better starting point.
What one wants to know, Maier concluded, should determine what theory to apply.

Juan Linz concurred with Maier, arguing that different theories explain different things. "Fascismustheorie" focuses on the movements themselves, especially
the inner core, and on the conditions that lead to the
success of those movements. "Fascismustheorie" is not
very helpful after Hitler took power, while the "totalitarian approach...[does have] something to say about how
the system worked when it was in power."

Linz stated that the legacies of anti-Semitism were incorporated into national fascisms in all cases, but that fascism itself does not necessarily involve racism. Once, however, Nazism became the dominant fascist movement, the symbol of fascism, it was "like a graft on a tree, and that branch grew so heavy and so great that it tore down the whole tree." The dilemma for late-coming fascist movements was to choose between the Italian and German models. The Nazi branch was a distinct one; many fascists were anti-Nazi, or at least suspicious of Nazism, Linz said. "Fascism would have been a much more successful world-European movement, and would have been more successful perhaps at surviving World War II, if it had been just Italian, and not Nazism."

Yet "the uniqueness of Nazism is compatible with the fascist approach," Linz maintained. Its uniqueness is accounted for by the particular characteristics of German social structure, of the organizational capacities of the state and so on. Linz cautioned that one should not exclude the charismatic role of Hitler within his party, or ignore his unique personality. But one should not reduce the Hitlerian state to the Führer alone, Linz said, for the Führer was surrounded by people that were loyal to him for various reasons. An explanation that "mythifies" Hitler deserves the kind of analysis that Marx gave in the critique of Victor Hugo on Napoleon Bonaparte: such an account renders its subject so great that it no longer makes sense.

Herbert Spiro highlighted the importance of the bureaucracy in German politics and the accompanying "administrative aversion to politics." Spiro traced the influence of this aversion as far as the theory of totalitarianism itself. The theory of totalitarianism, Spiro maintained, was a product of the context in which German intellectuals after the war found themselves, namely, the "messiness of American politics and society." Theorists of totalitarianism were "as much describing the constant flux, the uncertainty, the unpredictability...of their new home as they were the purported subject of their analysis," Spiro said. Spiro continued that totalitarian theory was "one of the most obscuring, obfuscating intellectual consequences of the Nazi experience; it has confused our concepts and introduced theories which are not very useful for purposes of analysis."

Thomas Childers concurred with Friedländer that anti-Bolshevism was secondary to anti-Semitism for Nazi leaders, but maintained that, in terms of the packaging and the appeals of the party, anti-Semitism was instrumental in the attacks on international finance and Marxism. German political culture was already steeped in anti-Semitism, Childers said. It was not an issue: it was respectable. The DDP and the SPD - parties one would have expected to rally against anti-Semitism - had a tendency to view it as a "fire made of straw." It would burn fast but go out quickly. In fact, German Communists and Conservatives alike believed that Hitler was actually more moderate than he appeared to be.

Dan White emphasized how important it was to address the puzzle of everyday life under Nazism: how could people believe that they led good lives, given the reality of the regime? White differed with Friedländer and with Levy's study on the meaning of decreased overt anti-Semitic activity before World War I and the six years after 1923. It was also observed from the floor that the reason a party, including an anti-Semitic one, becomes weaker is often that its program has become accepted by what were once more moderate parties.

Michael Kater emphasized the continuity of anti-Semitism, against what he saw as William Sheridan Allen's dictum that most people became anti-Semitic only after having become Nazi. Kater noted anti-Semitic outbreaks after the revolution of 1918, early in the 1920s, and in 1930-31 in Berlin. Kater also noted the ostracizing efforts of several social groups, notably, medical faculties and youth groups. The upper and middle classes, although perhaps not workers, were "permeated" with anti-Semitism, Kater said:

> a lot of ordinary Germans anticipated legislation on their own and did something to Jews at a very basic popular level that they had no business doing...I wonder why they did this. Doctors, for instance, made sure that their Jewish colleagues would be ousted from the profession before there was any legal precedent to do so.

Kater observed that historians addressed these issues shortly after the war, but have since tried to avoid them.

Jane Caplan noted that Nazi ideology was not limited exclusively to anti-Semitism. It also encompassed racism generally, as part of a whole imperial vision. Another aspect of Nazi racist ideology was the purification of the German race itself, Caplan said. This had consequences for how certain groups within Germany, including women and children, were treated.

Friedländer rejoined that historians have yet to identify what elements of anti-Semitism within the general population were specific to Germany, and could account for the rise of Hitler. Friedländer noted the lack of a systematic study of anti-Semitism during the Weimar period. On anti-Semitism within the Nazi regime itself, Friedländer maintained that it occupied a core position. It provides some but not all, clues about how the relations were structured between Hitler, other Nazi leaders and the population. "It was," Friedländer said, "a Sammelideologie (a catch-all politics) for everyone." Friedländer maintained that radicalism, for Hitler himself, was an outgrowth of anti-Semitism, even if, as Caplan had suggested, the reverse was the case for other Nazi leaders.

Mary Nolan outlined two different critiques of social democracy and associated welfare policies. One derives from Knut Borchardt's work: the welfare state was simply too expensive, it did not take account of the needs of industry. Nolan, however, argued that the requirements of capital are not quantifiable, as those requirements are determined in the realm of politics, not economics. Questioning the assumption that the working class was receiving too much and that welfare state demands contributed to the political crisis of late Weimar, Nolan suggested that the converse may have been the case; in other words, the welfare state served as a barrier to the working class's moving towards the right, Nolan said. It was the collapse of welfare provisions that delivered elements of the working class into the hands of the Nazis. The second criticism comes from the left: the SPD had a limited vision. In its own ideological confusion, on this view, the SPD clung to the image of the welfare state. Though commendable for its loyalty to the Republic, the SPD's response to rationalization and stabilization was shortsighted, Nolan said.

Nolan called for comparable analysis of industry. What was the vision of Germany that industrialists held? Was it achievable within the existing system? What was the relationship of industrialists to their pressure groups? What were industry's contributions to the crisis? Having underscored the importance of these questions, Nolan noted an apparent contradiction between Hamilton's study of voting and Turner's appraisal of business elites. Hamilton showed disproportionate elite votes for the Nazis: Turner argued that the elite was not pro-Nazi, Nolan said.

Richard Hamilton denied that a contradiction existed between his work and that of Turner. Hamilton noted that Turner's work covered several hundred individuals, while his own study encompassed several million people. Hamilton also noted that Turner had communicated to him that his subjects were generally still voting for "middle class" parties (such as the DVP, German People's Party) in 1932. Hamilton observed finally that the dependent variables differed in the two works: Turner examined financial support, while he himself concentrated on electoral support.

On the question of the burdens of the welfare state, Hamilton maintained that the economic cost of social spending and other provisions is indeed a researchable, quantifiable, issue. At the very least,

Hamilton said, one can make comparisons with other countries. Hamilton nevertheless urged that a study of the organization of businesses and their pressure groups be undertaken. Hamilton cautioned, however, that historians "ought to be ready to accept the conclusion that their organization had no payoff, that they were utter failures at what they tried to do."

David Abraham argued that the goal of the opponents of social democracy was not simply to strike down social welfare programs and to create better opportunities for business. Rather, the goal was to create "a fully authoritarian state, which would eliminate, altogether, the opportunity for these mistakes from ever happening again." "German business and economic groups clearly selected, altered, destroyed political parties in order that their demands came on the agenda when they did not have popular support," Abraham said.

Charles Maier noted that Germans in 1933 voted, "in a crazy way," for a return to normalcy, rather than apocalypse. German voters wanted "an end to being kicked around, an end to crisis, an end to the somewhere between fifteen and thirty parties competing for their votes, constant elections, Sunday brawls, an end to das System." Recalling the discussion on resistance and accommodation, Maier observed that "the dialectic of normalcy and apocalypse...remains the most intriguing aspect of National Socialism."

Stanley Hoffmann observed that the proceedings of the conference had highlighted several important cleavages in the study of history. Hoffmann noted the contributions of history "from the top" and history "from the bottom." Some historians emphasized the uniqueness of Nazism while others focused on similarities to other regimes. Hoffmann commented that historians working in functional areas, such as the economy and other "day-to-day" areas, drew parallels between Nazism and more "normal" regimes. Hoffmann mentioned the intentionalist and process approaches, as well as approaches that stress the will of the leader and those that highlight the occasional, intuition-oriented and discontinuous nature of leadership in the Third Reich. The Nazi experience reveals moral ambiguity to some historians, while others find ground for moral condemnation, said Hoffmann. And some students of the period center on the inevitability of various outcomes, while yet others point to choices and options open to historical actors.

Hoffmann said that Nazi ideology concentrated the poisons of nineteenth century thought. It was the particular combination of tradition and situation that caused Nazism to rise in Germany, rather than elsewhere, but the situation could always reappear.

152

NOTES

1. Zeëv Sternhell, Ni droite ni gauche: L'idéologie fasciste en France (Paris: Seuil, 1983).

2. Richard S. Levy, The Downfall of the Anti-Semitic Parties in Imperial Germany (New Haven: Yale University Press, 1975).

3. Ernst Nolte, Der Faschismus in seiner Epoche (Munich: Piper, 1963); English version, Three Faces of Fascism, Leila Vennewitz, trans. (New York: Holt, Rinehart, and Winston, 1966); Hans Mommsen, "Die Realisierung des Utopischen: Die 'Endlösung der Judenfrage' im 'Dritten Reich,'" Geschichte und Gesellschaft 9 (1983): 381-420. For Schieder's contribution, see the volume edited by Hans Mommsen, Totalitarismus und Fascismus. Eine wissenschaftliche Begriffskontroverse (Munich: Oldenbourg, 1980).

4. MacGregor Knox asserted later that "cumulative moderation" does not accurately describe events in Italy. What stopped Mussolini, Knox said, was the military defeat in 1940. Knox noted the steady growth in the internal and external claims made by the regime regarding Ethiopia in the late 1930s. The crucial difference between Italy and Germany, Knox said, was that Italy lacked both the resources and the military tradition upon which Germany drew so heavily.

5. The Berlin conference proceedings have appeared as Martin Broszat et al. eds., Deutschlands Weg in die Diktatur. Internationale Konferenz zur national-sozialistischen Machtübernahme im Reichstagsgebäude zu Berlin (Berlin: Siedler Verlag, 1984).

About the Contributors

ABRAHAM, David. The New School for Social Research, New York, N.Y.

ALLEN, William Sheridan. Department of History, State University of New York at Buffalo.

BENNETT, Edward W. Author of German Rearmament and the West, 1932-1933 (Princeton University Press, 1979).

CAPLAN, Jane. Department of History, Bryn Mawr College, Bryn Mawr, PA.

FRIEDLÄNDER, Saul. Department of Political Science, University of Tel Aviv, and Institut des Hautes Etudes Internationales, Geneva.

GEYER, Michael. Department of History, University of Michigan, Ann Arbor.

GOULD, Andrew. Department of Political Science, University of California at Berkeley.

HERF, Jeffrey. Center for International Affairs, Harvard University, and Department of Political Science, The College of the Holy Cross, Worcester, MA.

HOFFMANN, Stanley. Department of Government and Center for European Studies, Harvard University.

KATER, Michael H. Department of History, York University, Toronto.

KOONZ, Claudia. Department of History, The College of the Holy Cross, Worcester, MA.

MAIER, Charles S. Department of History and Center for European Studies, Harvard University.

RABINBACH, Anson. Department of History, Cooper Union Institute, New York, NY.

ROVAN, Joseph. Institut d'Allemagne, Université de Paris, III.

TENFELDE, Klaus. History faculty, University of Munich.